DON'T BE AFRAID

GERALD M. ROSEN, Ph. D. was at the University of Oregon for three years as a Visiting Assistant Professor and Research Associate. He is now a clinical psychologist in private practice and is Chief Psychologist at Providence Medical Center in Seattle, Washington.

DON'T BE AFRAID

A Program for Overcoming Your Fears and Phobias

GERALD M. ROSEN

A SPECTRUM BOOK

PRENTICE-HALL, INC., Englewood Cliffs, New Jersey 07632

Library of Congress Cataloging in Publication Data

Rosen, Gerald,
  Don't be afraid.

  (A Spectrum Book)
  Bibliography: p.
  1. Fear.   2. Phobias.   I. Title.
BF575.F2R67   152.4'34   76-40290
ISBN 0-13-218404-4
isbn 0-13-218404-4 pbk.

A Spectrum Book

10 9 8 7 6 5 4 3 2 1

Printed in the United States of America

Prentice-Hall International, Inc., *London*
Prentice-Hall of Australia Pty. Limited, *Sydney*
Prentice-Hall of Canada, Ltd., *Toronto*
Prentice-Hall of India Private Limited, *New Delhi*
Prentice-Hall of Japan, Inc., *Tokyo*
Prentice-Hall of Southeast Asia Pte. Ltd., *Singapore*
Whitehall Books Limited, *Wellington, New Zealand*

Acknowledgements

I thank Drs. HERBERT ORENSTEIN, JOHN REID, and ALAN MARLATT. The opportunity to complete this book and related research was made possible by their friendship and support.

To my wife, Betsy
. . . and the ship's voyage

CONTENTS

1

IS THIS BOOK FOR YOU?

Think of any object or situation and you can probably find someone afraid of it. People get tense and feel anxious about medical procedures, dentists, heights, storms, the dark, airplanes, and driving cars. They have fears of insects and animals ranging from stinging bees and harmless ladybugs to poisonous snakes and the neighborhood dog. Situations that upset many people include meetings with in-laws, speaking in public, job interviews, and social dates. The full list of everyday things that make people tense, anxious, or fearful may very well be endless.

This book is for people who are willing to conduct their own treatment to overcome commonly occurring fears and tensions. The book presents a program that you can successfully apply at home. It can be used for all the fears listed above and for other fears as well. In fact, the procedures are adaptable to just about any object or situation that causes you discomfort.

This book can also be used to treat very severe fears or phobias. The term *phobia* is used when people have such strong fears that they actively avoid those things which upset them. There is another important point to consider before labeling a person's fear reactions as phobic. In the case of phobia, a person gets tense and anxious toward things that are **not** really harmful. Thus, a person who crosses streets to avoid a pet poodle on a leash is acting in a phobic manner. People are not phobic when they avoid a dog that they know has bitten people on past occasions.

Whether you use this book to treat mild fears or more severe phobias, you will be interested to know that this type of program has actually been tested by professionals in controlled studies. You can find a complete listing of relevant references in the back of this book. *In every case*, published reports show that people can successfully apply their own treatment program. Although research findings are certainly positive, one must realize that self-administered treatments are by no means a cure-all. Just as aspirin can only treat some headaches, so does the present program have its limitations. To decide if *you* are likely to be helped by this book, you should consider two issues.

The first issue of primary concern is your motivation. Studies on self-administered treatments show that as many as 50 percent of the participants fail to complete their programs. These individuals often blame environmental factors such as their being sick, moving, or changing jobs. Although explanations like these sound reasonable, most of the time they are really excuses. When something is important enough, people find the time to get it done.

It turns out that some people aren't sufficiently motivated when it comes to treating their own fears and phobias. One reason for this is that living with a fear is not always a problem. For example, if you lived in New York City and were afraid of snakes, there would be little opportunity to be inconvenienced by your fear. There may be a dozen reasons why walking in New

York isn't safe, but chancing upon a snake in downtown Manhattan isn't one of them!

Of course, many people find living with a fear or phobia a real and difficult problem that affects everyday functioning. While snake phobics get along in New York, a mother in Oregon who is afraid of snakes and who refuses to go camping will disappoint her children and miss out on family activities. An elevator phobic in the country can get to the top of small-town buildings by walking up stairs; a person with similar fears in a city filled with skyscrapers is more severely inconvenienced. At times, the restriction of activities due to a severe phobia can be highly incapacitating. Many people who are afraid of going out alone or being in public places (agoraphobia) find it impossible to enjoy even the simplest activities outside their homes.

As a general rule, people are motivated to change when they are inconvenienced by their fears. With this in mind, you should consider how great a problem your fear or phobia is to you. How motivated are you to work through this treatment program? Think about this issue now to avoid getting involved in something you never intend to finish. This treatment program involves at least two forty-minute sessions each week for as many as six to eight weeks. Can you spend that much time to eliminate a troublesome fear or to reduce your anxiety in uncomfortable situations?

Once you decide how motivated you are, you need to think about the second issue: What kind of a problem do you have? The program in this book is probably most effective when anxiety and fears are focused on specific objects or situations. An example of what this means is provided by Mr. J., who has feared medical procedures since he underwent an operation twenty years ago. At times, Mr. J.'s anxiety is so severe that he refuses to see a doctor when medical treatment is clearly needed. He knows his fear is unrealistic, but the thought of blood, injections, and even the doctor's office are highly upsetting. If you ask Mr. J. about himself, he tells you his fear has little, if anything, to do with the rest of his life. It happens that Mr. J. is also anxious about heights, but there is no relation between this fear and his anxiety toward doctors.

Would Mr. J. be a good candidate for the program in this book? The answer is definitely yes. Mr. J.'s fear of doctors is focused on a specific situation which bears little relation to other areas of his life. The fact that Mr. J. is also afraid of heights is not important. His two fears are easily distinguished from each other, and they appear to be separate problems. As a matter of fact, Mr. J. could use the treatment program twice. He could first treat himself for his medical phobia, then he could apply the same procedures to his fear of heights. Mr. J. would have an excellent chance of substantially reducing *both* fears if he was motivated to work through the entire program.

If your fears are specific, like Mr. J.'s, you will probably benefit from this book. That doesn't mean you have to be afraid of medical procedures and heights; your fear can relate to most any object of situation imaginable. It also doesn't matter how fearful you are. You can be severely phobic and never get near what bothers you. Or you can be the kind of person who gets things done but wants to feel less tense and uncomfortable. The important point is not *what* you fear or *how* fearful you may be. The relevant issue concerns the extent to which your fear is focused on particular objects or situations and the ways in which your fear relates to other areas of your life.

Another case example can further clarify this discussion. Consider Mr. S., who is also afraid of medical procedures and who has avoided doctors for many years. For Mr. S. there are numerous reasons why visiting a doctor is distressing. Mr. S. dislikes traveling anywhere away from home; so he feels anxious driving across town to the doctor's office. He is also generally tense in social situations; so he is uncomfortable when he interacts with the receptionist and nurses. If you ask Mr. S. about himself, he tells you that he often feels upset; visiting the doctor is but one example of a more general problem. Mr. S. is unable to specify what causes him trouble because his anxiety is generalized to so many different objects and situations.

Mr. S. is the kind of person who might have difficulty applying on his own the program in this book. Because he is generally unhappy and feels anxious in almost all areas of his life, Mr. S. is likely to benefit most from the personal guidance of a professional counselor, someone who can help Mr. S. define the specific things that upset him. With the help of a professional, Mr. S. could then use the present program to treat those fears that had been clearly defined and associated with particular situations and objects.

You can now decide if this treatment program is for you. Be objective and make the right decision for yourself. First, ask yourself if eliminating your fears and anxieties is an important goal. Will you invest the time needed to complete your program? Next, ask yourself if your fears and anxieties are related to specific objects and situations. Are other problem areas in your life separate from the specific fears you want to work on, or are you generally unhappy and confused about the sources of your tension? *If you are motivated and can clearly define your fears and anxieties, then you are likely to find this book very beneficial.*

One last point. This program does not encourage you to do things that make you too uncomfortable. So don't read every page anxiously concerned about what happens next. Try to relax as much as possible. Enjoy the book. Adopt a new attitude toward your feelings: develop a curiosity about fears and the ways they can be changed. Learning new things about yourself and overcoming a fear or phobia can be an interesting and rewarding experience.

In the next two chapters you will learn more about the nature of fears and how people eliminate them. Then your program starts and you will begin the process of reducing your anxiety. As you work on your treatment, please remember— there is nothing to be afraid of!

2

SOME FACTS ABOUT
FEARS AND PHOBIAS

Many people are embarrassed by a fear or phobia. They wonder what is wrong with them, and they hide their feelings from friends and relatives. The information in this chapter should dispel any myths you may hold about your fears. You will see that there is nothing mysterious about feeling tense and anxious, it doesn't mean you are "crazy" or "disturbed," and there is nothing to be embarrassed about.

People are often surprised to learn that fears and phobias are rather common. In one survey conducted by researchers at the University of Vermont, almost 1 in 10 persons interviewed were judged to be suffering from a serious fear. If milder anxiety problems were tabulated, the percentage figures would likely be higher. Most common among the reported phobias were fears of medical procedures, dentists, heights, storms, snakes, and flying in airplanes. The full list of specific things people feared was much longer.

The investigators at Vermont studied a number of the identified phobics for five years to learn more about the natural course of phobias. The results from their study showed that most childhood phobias were short-lived and subsided on their own. This finding may be similar to your own experiences if you have raised children. One year your child is afraid of the dark, the next year dogs, and the next year there is yet another concern.

Unlike the fears of childhood, adult phobias persist. Over half the adult phobics in the Vermont study had failed to improve during the five-year period. Thirty-three percent of these individuals actually experienced an increase in the severity of their fears.

Findings from the Vermont survey tell us that adult phobias occur frequently and they are persistent. But what does it mean to say someone has a fear or a phobia? The following examples will show you that there is no simple answer to this question. *Fear and phobia mean different things to different people.*

Mrs. Swanson is terrified of snakes. She refuses to visit parks or go on walks by herself for fear that a snake lies hidden in the grass. Mrs. Swanson is so fearful that when a snake turns up on her television screen, she screams and runs out of the room. When that happens, her breath gets short and her heart starts pounding against her chest.

Unlike Mrs. Swanson, Frank Brenner says he has no fears worth mentioning. Yet, when you bring him into a room and show him a pet rat, he refuses to approach the animal. He says he would prefer to stay away—although he really isn't afraid. You convince Frank to approach the rat just a little. When he does and you take his pulse, you see that his heartbeat is unusually fast.

James Turner is a college student majoring in English literature. James hopes to be a teacher one day, but he is anxious about speaking in public. The last time he talked to a group of people, he experienced a dry mouth and his hands perspired heavily. On several occasions he lost track of his thoughts and stumbled over his words. The experience was so upsetting that James has been unwilling to speak in public ever since.

Mr. Faulkner has been looking for a job for the past three months. About six weeks ago, during an interview, he suddenly felt "butterflies" in his stomach. By the time the interview was over, Mr. Faulkner's stomach was in knots. He has continued to feel tense during subsequent interviews, but he continues to go in hopes of finding employment.

Sally Fairburn responded to a questionnaire about fears and reported being "extremely afraid" of spiders. To test the extent of her fear she was asked to approach a large spider securely enclosed in a glass cage. Much to her surprise, Sally walked up to the cage, lifted its cover, and put her hand near the spider. Her pulse was perfectly normal while she did all this, and she did not report other signs of physical tension. Later, Sally insisted she had been afraid during the test.

The people in these case examples are all *talking, feeling* or *acting*, in ways that indicate they are anxious. To some extent, they each appear to have a fear or a phobia. But consider the differences among these five people. Some directly experienced physical tension, while others did not. Even those who had strong physical reactions differed from each other. Mrs. Swanson experienced her heart beating, while Mr. Faulkner felt muscle tension in his stomach.

The self-reports of these individuals also differed, as did the ways they actually behaved in stress situations. Sally reported that she was terrified of spiders, but she still approached one in a test setting. Mr. Brenner insisted he was not afraid of anything, but then refused to go near a pet rat.

Seeming contradictions like these are observed all the time among people with fears and phobias. But psychologists have come to realize that the differences are not contradictory at all. They simply mean that there really is no *one* thing that can be called a fear or a phobia. Instead, the terms *fear* or *phobia* are descriptive words that cover a variety of reactions to stressful events. The terms tell us that *something* related to anxiety is occurring—exactly what that means will differ from one person to the next.

Take some time to consider how these points apply to your behavior. What is it that makes you feel anxious and fearful? Would you characterize your reactions as being "slightly anxious," "moderately afraid," or "extremely upset?" How you describe what you fear and the extent of your reactions represents a *verbal report* of your feelings.

Now, what would you actually do if you came across the thing that upsets you? Remember that two people with identical verbal reports can act very differently when confronted by the thing they fear. Are you the kind of person who would freeze on the spot? Would you turn and run? Would you muster all your courage and stay in the situation? Or would you do something else? Whatever you would do, your reactions represent *overt behaviors.*

You can also consider how your body internally reacts to stress. Does your heart pound? Do you get knots or butterflies in your stomach? Do you perspire, feel dizzy, or breathe rapidly? People with identical verbal reports and overt behaviors can still have individualized body reactions to stress. How you react represents your *physiological responses.*

Verbal reports, overt behaviors, and physiological responses constitute the talking, acting, and feeling components of fear. It is interesting to consider how social factors may explain why the components of fear vary so greatly from one person to the next. For example, men are less likely than women to report a fear or phobia. Is this because men are truly less fearful, or are they less willing to publicly admit having fears? In addition to social factors, individual responses to stress are influenced by heredity. Experiments have shown that genetic factors affect our physical reactions to stress even during infancy.

Individual differences in stress reactions are probably caused by still other factors yet to be identified. For the time being, we can only observe that differences do exist and consider the implications of these differences for the question "What does having a fear or a phobia mean?" You should now be able to give an accurate answer to this question. First, you will want to object to the very wording of the question itself. People don't "have" fears or phobias like they would "have" a common cold. The terms *fear* and *phobia* simply describe three kinds of behaviors: verbal (talking), overt (acting), and physical (feeling). We say that people are fearful when they either report anxiety, avoid things and act frightened, experience physical reactions associated with tension—or have any combination of these three events. Because people have individualized reactions to stress, the relationships between verbal, overt, and physical responses vary. One individual may report anxiety even while walking all the way up to a feared object and showing no physical signs of distress. Another individual may report only slight anxiety but experience stomach tightness and refuse to even step toward the feared object.

Defining fears and phobias in terms of specific behaviors makes it easier to discuss an important question: "How did your fears develop?" Hopefully it is clear by now that you do not have a mysterious disease or illness. What you do have are behaviors or "ways of experiencing" things. And these have been learned for one reason or another. Why did *you* learn these behaviors? In some cases, people are tense and anxious as a result of psychologically traumatic and highly upsetting accidents. This is why people are often unwilling to fly in airplanes or ride in cars; they have been in accidents themselves or know someone else who has. In cases like these, people vividly remember how their fear was learned.

Other people learn their fears from significant friends or relatives. For example, a sizable number of people afraid of bees, spiders, or other insects report having mothers with similar fears. These individuals clearly recall their mothers crying or running out of the room when a bug was spotted. Unwittingly, the parents served as "models" and taught their fears to their children.

It is intriguing to speculate that innate or inborn factors may also influence the development of fears and phobias. In support of this position is evidence that we are predisposed to react with anxiety in certain situations. You may have observed that children invariably go through a stage when they fear all strangers. It has also been demonstrated that infants show an inborn avoidance of cliffs or other steep heights.

The uniform tendency of infants and children to respond anxiously to particular kinds of situations suggests the influence of innate behavioral tendencies. Such tendencies may explain why some fears are more prevalent than others. At the same time, it is important to keep the role of inherited factors in their proper perspective. Whatever may be our initial tendencies or innate fear reactions, they are significantly reshaped by our experiences in life. That is why as adults, most of us are no longer afraid of heights or anxious when we first meet people.

Many of you are unlikely to remember specific events or people that have influenced the development of your fears. This is to be expected, since many fears probably result from a series of minor or trivial incidents. You should also realize that people with fears may not have any relevant experiences to remember. In fact, anxieties and fear can result from a *lack of experience!* Take people who are anxious when they go to a job interview. Their fear doesn't have to relate to a traumatic experience; nor does it have to result from living with an anxious person. Instead, people can be anxious simply because they have never been interviewed for a job before; they don't know what to expect or how to act.

As you can see, fears and phobias develop for a variety of reasons. What they all share in common is this: they are learned behaviors that relate to past experiences . . . or lack of such.

TREATING FEARS AND PHOBIAS

Some believe that a person must understand the origins of a problem to bring about meaningful change. However, most professionals now agree that "understanding" alone is not enough to relieve your anxious feelings. You can probably think of examples yourself that demonstrate this point. Perhaps you are afraid to drive cars because you were once the victim of a near-fatal accident. While you know that your anxiety developed because of a particular incident, you are still unable to drive. A friend of yours may be afraid of doctors because her mother used to scream when receiving an injection. Has the knowledge that her mother taught her to be afraid helped your friend reduce her fear? An individual I worked with was afraid of snakes. When she was a child her brother used to hold a snake in his hand and teasingly chase her around the house. We both agreed that her brother had a poor sense of humor, but this did little to help the problem.

These examples illustrate a point you may have already known: the factors that cause fears and the best way to treat fears are two rather separate matters. If you think you understand how your fears developed, that's fine. You may remember a traumatic experience, a series of unpleasant episodes, or an influential person in your life. Many of you won't remember a reason for your fears, and that's also OK. Either way, you are dealing with learned behaviors that bear a relation to past experiences; either way, you can change your fears and reduce your anxiety.

Let's step back now and take a second look at the nature of the problem with which you are dealing. As you have seen, fears and phobias are learned ways of talking, acting, and feeling. The University of Vermont survey demonstrated that these kinds of behaviors tend to persist among adults. This finding raises the question, "Why do fears and phobias persist?" It turns out that this is an important question because its answer provides an insight into how fears and phobias can be overcome.

To find out why fears and phobias persist, let's consider the "typical experiences" of an "average fearful person." Mr. T., a man afraid of the dark, will serve as our example. Mr. T. copes with his fear by avoiding situations in which there are no lights. He stays at home evenings, and always keeps a light on, even when asleep. Unfortunately, there are times when it is difficult to avoid the dark. The most distressing example of this occurs when a nighttime thunderstorm knocks down the electrical power lines to his country home. When this happens, Mr. T. gets anxious and his body tenses up. He runs from room to room lighting kerosene lamps and candles as quickly as he can. Only after the house is fully lighted does he feel well again.

Let's look at the sequence of these events. First, Mr. T. is at home feeling his usual self. Then a storm knocks out the electricity, and he is confronted with the very thing he most fears—total darkness. Not unexpectedly, he immediately feels distressed. In technical terms we say that *exposure* to the feared object or situation has *increased anxiety*.

Mr. T. tries to terminate the exposure as quickly as possible: lighting his home makes him feel better. This illustrates how the *termination of exposure* can *decrease anxiety*. The full sequence of events looks like this:

| *Exposure* to the feared object or situation | → | *Distress:* Increased anxiety | → | *Termination of* exposure | → | *Relief:* Decreased anxiety |

You can probably apply Mr. T.'s behavior to your own situation. First, you are likely to make every effort to avoid the situation or object that upsets you. When this is not feasible, you are likely to terminate exposure as rapidly as possible. The same thing happens to the woman who fears worms and sees one on television: she suddenly feels upset . . . she closes her eyes or leaves the room . . . then she feels better. The man afraid to talk to women approaches them infrequently, when conversations are unavoidable, he quickly ends them: his early termination of conversations brings relief.

As it turns out, brief exposure contacts can cause fears to persist. Think about this for a moment. All of a sudden you are faced with the very thing you fear. You are reminded how it really is upsetting: *Exposure* leads to *distress.* It is only natural to then try to terminate exposure as quickly as possible. But watch how you end up confirming your *need* to escape. Reductions in anxiety and relief from distress occur only after you get away. In effect, you learn that *terminating exposure* leads to *relief.* You now see how you can do things in such a way that you unwittingly confirm your fears. You learn to associate exposure with distress, termination with relief. The message is: "I really am afraid and I have to get away." In this way a vicious cycle is established in which your fears are actually maintained by your attempts to avoid anxiety.

Let's consider what would happen if we altered the usual sequence of events. (Note: the following example is *not* how this program works. So try to understand the points *without* getting upset.) What if we took Mr. T. and surprised him in the following way. Suppose while he was away at work, we hid all his kerosene lamps, candles, and matches and disconnected the fuse box so that electricity no longer reached his house. And suppose that when Mr. T. returned home we locked all the doors and windows so that he couldn't get out. For Mr. T. this would certainly be a surprise—and a terrifying one at that. As night fell and his house became totally dark, he would be trapped in the very situation he most wanted to avoid.

What would happen to Mr. T. as he remained trapped in his darkened home? Obviously, he would become tremendously upset. He would feel miserable because we had cut off the last half of the sequence: we had prevented him from escaping and terminating exposure. Mr. T. would now be experiencing this:

Exposure to the feared object or situation	*Distress:* Increased anxiety	*Can't terminate* exposure	*Increased distress*
→	→	→	

Although Mr. T.'s anxiety would continue to rise, something else would eventually happen that isn't immediately obvious. If enough time elapsed, Mr. T.'s anxiety would eventually decrease. It is important to underline the words *enough time.* It could take several hours, or even several nights, before Mr. T.'s tension decreased. But however long it took, there would *eventually* occur a reduction in anxiety.

To some extent this inevitable decrease in Mr. T.'s anxiety could result from plain fatigue. A person can stay anxious for just so long before exhaustion sets in. However, other factors are likely to be at work. As the hours passed, Mr. T. would realize he was *not* dying; none of the terrible things he always feared would happen would be happening. For the first time in his life, Mr. T. would be staying around long enough to see that his fears and anxieties were unjustified. In effect, a new sequence of events would occur.

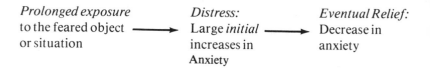

Prolonged exposure	*Distress:*	*Eventual Relief:*
to the feared object →	Large *initial* →	Decrease in
or situation	increases in	anxiety
	Anxiety	

Compare the above sequence involving prolonged exposure to the more typical course of events:

Exposure to the	*Distress:*	*Termination of*	*Relief:*
feared object →	Increased →	exposure →	Decreased
or situation	anxiety		anxiety

Notice that both sequences lead to an eventual reduction in anxiety. In this sense, both sequences give Mr. T. exactly what he wants. The problem with prolonged exposure is that a person has to experience intense suffering before relief is felt. Mr. T. would have gone through hell if he had been trapped in his darkened house. Only after an extended period of time would he have felt better.

Despite the discomfort, prolonged exposure has one important advantage: it actually helps people overcome their fears and phobias. To understand why this is so, consider the typical or "natural" sequence of events that maintains your own fears. In the typical situation, exposure leads to anxiety, and escape leads to relief. In this way relief occurs only *after* exposure is terminated. With prolonged exposure the situation is very different. After an initial increase in anxiety, a reduction in tension occurs *while* exposure is maintained. *For the first time, relief is associated with the presence of the object or situation that is feared.* It is then possible to learn that terrible things don't have to happen during exposure: *it is possible not to be afraid.* Therapists have developed prolonged-exposure procedures that successfully eliminate fears and phobias. But without a therapist's supervision, it is unrealistic to ask people (like yourself) to self-administer this approach. Subjecting yourself to prolonged exposure requires your doing what most upsets you. Once in the feared situation, your anxiety would build up and you would feel increasingly distressed. Finally, the experience would become too much to bear, and you would do the very thing we have seen maintains fear—escape. The only way to avoid this would be to "lock the door and throw away the key." And who wants to do that to themselves?

Self-administered procedures based on prolonged exposure are thus unrealistic. If you were reading the last few pages shuddering at the thought—*don't worry!* This book does *not* ask you to practice any distressful procedures; you will *not* have to do anything that makes you too uncomfortable.

If you won't be practicing prolonged exposure, then why discuss this issue at such length? Earlier I said that understanding why fears and phobias persist provides an insight into how these problems can be solved. You have learned that fears and phobias persist because exposure leads to anxiety and escape brings relief. Our discussion of prolonged exposure demonstrates that methods other than escape can lead to relief. It turns out that a *general principle* of fear reduction underlies this specific technique:

> *Feeling comfortable while exposure*
> *is maintained can help you overcome*
> *your fear or phobia.*

This principle is the key to all successful treatments of fears and phobias. In the next chapter you will learn how to apply the principle to *your* self-administered program.

3

YOUR TREATMENT PROGRAM

Imagine a woman—Jane—standing about eight feet from the edge of a swimming pool. Jane is afraid of the water and so she stands far enough away to remain comfortable. All of a sudden, her husband comes up from behind, lifts her up, and throws her into the pool. He has decided to try on his wife the old "sink or swim" approach to fear reduction.

You now know enough about fears and phobias to predict what will happen. The most likely sequence of events is that Jane becomes tremendously anxious and gets out of the pool as fast as she can. This experience will teach her just the wrong things: she will learn that being in the water makes her anxious and that escaping from the water brings relief. Her husband's efforts at fear reduction will have backfired.

Of course, if her husband prevented Jane from escaping, we would have a situation involving prolonged exposure. And if enough time elapsed, we would expect an eventual decrease in

Jane's anxiety. Unfortunately, there would also be a decrease in Jane's attachment to her husband who forced her into the uncomfortable situation!

Can people overcome a fear or phobia without experiencing prolonged exposure and severe distress? In the preceding chapter you were told that the key to all successful treatments is the principle:

Feeling comfortable while exposure
is maintained can help you overcome
your fear or phobia.

It turns out that there is a way you can apply this principle and overcome your fears *without* major distress. First, let us assume there are actions or experiences *opposed* to anxiety. For example, you cannot be tense and anxious at the same time that you are feeling very relaxed and comfortable. Now, what if you took part in a special training program and learned how to consciously relax away muscle tension in your body? You would then know how to do something that was incompatible with tension and discomfort.

The next question would be: how could you use your newly acquired relaxation skills to reduce a fear or phobia? Remember that the basic principle for successful treatment involves feeling comfortable while exposure is maintained. If you learned to relax, you would know how to feel comfortable; so the trick is to find a way to maintain exposure while feeling relaxed. Prolonged exposure is clearly *not* the way to do this. But what if instead you *gradually* approached the thing you feared? In that way you would never need to experience uncomfortable tension at any step in your program. To see how this can be accomplished, let's go back and consider Jane's situation. Assume that Jane has completed a course in muscle relaxation. She is again standing about eight feet from the pool's edge while watching her husband and children enjoy the water. Jane wishes she could join them, but the thought of entering the water makes her anxious. She realizes, however, that she *could* take three steps toward the pool without feeling more than slightly tense. Now that she knows how to relax her muscles, Jane is confident she could eliminate small increases in tension. Accordingly, Jane takes three steps forward and actively works at relaxing away her discomfort. Within a few minutes she is familiar with the situation and feels comfortable.

Naturally, Jane is still afraid of walking up to the very edge of the pool—not to mention getting into the water. But Jane has successfully eliminated one stage of her anxiety: she can stand closer to the pool and remain comfortable. The sequence of events looks like this:

Gradual exposure to the feared object or situation	→	*Slight discomfort countered by relaxation*	→	*Relief* in the practiced situation

Once Jane has become comfortable standing only five feet from the pool, she can think of the next step in her approach. It occurs to Jane that going forward another three steps would cause a good deal of anxiety. After all, every step is bringing her that much closer to the water. Jane wants to avoid approaching the pool too quickly since large increases in anxiety would be difficult or impossible to relax away. Therefore, she decides to approach the pool again—but this time only two steps more. After staying in the situation for a few minutes and concentrating on relaxing her muscles, Jane is finally comfortable standing only three feet from the pool.

Notice how Jane is able to progressively approach the pool without experiencing any real discomfort. This is because she is gradually approaching in a systematic, step-by-step manner. Originally, Jane would have never felt comfortable standing only three feet from the pool's edge. But the first successful experience of walking toward the water has made the second stage of her approach easier to handle. In this way, Jane can gradually eliminate her fear without ever feeling uncontrollably tense. Jane has found a new way to apply the basic principle for fear reduction. *She is maintaining exposure through gradual approach while at the same time remaining comfortable by relaxing her muscles.*

You can probably anticipate the remaining steps in Jane's program. Next, she might walk all the way up to the pool's edge. She could then get into the water up to her ankles. Eventually, Jane could learn to swim and really enjoy the pool. Let's outline the procedural steps that Jane has followed:

1. Jane first needed to know how to relax her muscles. Learning this skill provided her with a response opposed to anxiety.

2. Jane then had to plan a strategy for *gradually* approaching the pool. Properly planning this strategy is critical for a successful program. Jane never wanted to approach too fast, since this would have caused too much anxiety. She tried to plan each stage of her program so that she would only have to relax away small amounts of tension.

3. Jane combined the first two parts of the program by gradually approaching the pool and using her relaxation skills to oppose slight increases in anxiety or tension.

4. Whenever Jane became comfortable at a stage of her program, she moved on to the next stage. Each successful experience made subsequent steps easier to master.

If you think about it for a moment, the program that Jane followed is rather straightforward. Why is it that people with fears and phobias haven't already tried these procedures on their own? One reason is that most people don't know how to adequately relax their muscles. Learning this is a definite skill that takes special training and practice.

A second reason people don't try gradual approach is that the idea rarely occurs to them. Most people with fears and phobias are always busy trying to *avoid* the object or situation that upsets them. On those rare occasions when people approach the thing they fear, they are determined to "conquer the problem" once and for all. And when people think like that, the notion of gradual approach would never do! A man who decides to finally conquer his fear of driving doesn't just sit in his car, or drive only the length of his driveway. Instead, he tries to drive an unrealistically long distance and totally master the situation. A woman afraid of job interviews doesn't think of practicing an interview with her friends, or having an interview for a job she doesn't really care about. Instead, she plunges ahead and interviews for the most important job of her life. Unfortunately, when people try to overcome fears "all at once," they usually experience a distressing amount of anxiety—the upsetting experience only causes them to remain fearful.

Thus, people have natural tendencies which help to explain why they rarely attempt gradual approach on their own. Of course, people *can* change these tendencies, and people *can* learn to deeply relax their muscles—and (if you haven't already guessed) that's *exactly* what *you* are going to do. Your treatment program is going to teach you how to gradually approach the thing you fear while remaining calm and relaxed. Now, some people will immediately say to themselves, "Oh, no, I could never do that. I could never approach what I fear." If you feel this way, reconsider the actual procedures involved. Remember that you will first learn how to relax. This is a useful skill that is enjoyable to develop. After learning to fully relax your body muscles, you will plan a strategy for gradually approaching the object or situation that is feared. To do this, you will create a list of situations or scenes that can gradually increase your exposure to the thing that upsets you. You will not actually *do* any of these things—you will only *plan* your strategy.

After you have learned to relax and have planned your strategy for approach, you will combine the two procedures and work on overcoming your fear or phobia. By practicing the program one step at a time, and by starting with the *easiest* situations, you will never have to practice anything that makes you too anxious. The following examples can help you see more clearly how this is possible.

Imagine that you have taught yourself to relax and are now

planning your strategy for gradual approach. If you are afraid of flying in airplanes, you might decide to do sixteen or twenty things that gradually lead up to being on a plane. You might first look at pictures of planes, then go to an airport just to see them. If going to an airport makes you too anxious, you might first call an airport and get accustomed to speaking about flight times and ticket costs. It might also be useful to visit a travel agent. The exact details of a program require careful planning, and a rather lengthy chapter (Chapter 5) will teach you how to set yours up. But you can see now that your approach can be gradual; you will be able to feel comfortable at each step in your program.

If you are afraid of the dark, you might start off by staying in the dark with some friends. If that makes you too anxious, you could begin your program in a dimly lit room. People still uncomfortable with this could simply look at pictures of dark rooms. Alternatively, a person could stay in a well-lit room while standing ten feet away from a dark closet. If that created too much anxiety, the person could stand fifteen feet away.

The point of the above examples is that there will always be something you *can* do, and that is where you will start your program. The unusual and sometimes ingenious ways you can go about approaching and conquering your fears will be outlined in Chapter 5. The important thing to realize for now, is that you *will* be able to do it—and you *will not* have to suffer.

The remainder of this book is divided into three sections, each dealing with a step in your program. In Step 1 you will learn how to relax your muscles. Once you master these procedures you will be able to reduce many minor everyday tensions and you will know how to use your muscles more efficiently. Most importantly, you will have developed an important new skill for overcoming your fears and phobias.

In the chapter after relaxation training you will plan your strategy for gradually approaching the object or situation that you fear (Step 2). Then, in Step 3, you will learn the rules for combining relaxation skills with gradual approach. Naturally, these rules are important to follow, and you will want to study them carefully

SOME IMPORTANT POINTS BEFORE
YOU BEGIN

The remaining chapters teach you how to self-administer an effective treatment program. To be successful, you will need to study each chapter and practice the various procedures described. While that probably doesn't come as any surprise, there are a few points to keep in mind.

First, be sure to study each chapter in its proper order. Never skip ahead out of curiosity to see what is coming up next. After all, if you were working with a therapist in his private office, you would certainly follow the treatment program step by step. Only after you had successfully completed the first part of the procedures would your therapist present the second part. You would not be able to skip from one section to the next because your therapist would systematically guide you through the treatment. *You should allow your written treatment program to systematically guide you through the procedures just as a therapist would.* Only after all the materials in a particular chapter are mastered should you proceed to a new section of instructions.

A second point to consider is the structuring of your program: When will you work on the procedures, and how will you schedule sessions? My experience with people who self-administer their treatment has demonstrated this to be the *most* critical issue. Just consider the following two situations to see why this is so:

SITUATION 1: Sarah has an appointment with a very busy doctor in town. She has been waiting all week to see the doctor and she really wants to get some help for her problem. The appointment is set for Friday afternoon at four o'clock. Thursday night a man Sarah wants to see calls and suggests going to a late afternoon movie and dinner. What does Sarah do?

Does she say she can't make the date because she has a very important appointment, but she would like to get together some other time? Or does Sarah figure she can always get an appointment for some other time, say yes to the date, and go to the movies?

SITUATION 2: Sarah has scheduled a session for herself to work on her self-administered program. She has been waiting all week to hold this session, and she really wants to work on her problem. The session is scheduled for Friday afternoon at four o'clock. Thursday night a man that Sarah would like to see calls and suggests going to a late afternoon movie and dinner. Again, what does Sarah do?

What Sarah is likely to do in the above two situations is all too clear, and you can now see the problem. When you have an appointment with a busy doctor, you tend to be responsible and keep it. Unfortunately, it is more difficult to stick to your plans when you don't have this "outside" support. Appointments with yourself can always be put off—but when you put off your self-administered appointments, you never complete your program. So beware: don't fall into the trap! When planning to work on your program, treat *all* sessions as official appointments that really need to be kept. Try not to break them. If you are ill or can't make a session for some other good reason, show yourself the same courtesy you would extend to a doctor—*reschedule* for a new time.

A good way to structure your work is to schedule regular session times. Most people find it convenient to hold two sessions each week, but you can hold more if you want. Allow for a few days between sessions. For example, if one session is on Monday, have the next session on Thursday or Friday, not on Tuesday. Naturally, if you hold more than two sessions each week, the time between sessions will decrease.

Since your program begins in the next chapter, this is a good time to decide when to regularly meet with yourself. Pick at least two times per week that are likely to remain convenient during the next eight weeks. Also figure on your sessions taking between thirty and forty minutes. After you decide on your times, write them down on the next page.

	Session 1	Session 2	Session 3 or more (optional)
WEEKLY MEETING:	_____	_____	_____
	Day, time	Day, time	Day, time

Now write the times you have chosen on your calendar. Remember each week to keep your appointments just as if you were seeing a therapist. There are a few additional points to cover, and then you can begin your program. In some chapters there will be a short series of questions to assess your mastery of the materials. When you come across one of these "quizzes," treat the questions seriously and see how many you can really answer. If you get a question wrong, it means you should go back and study the instructions more carefully.

You will also find in some chapters a number of pages called "Log Sheets." These provide a place for keeping track of your sessions and what is being working on. Most people find the sheets extremely helpful, and you should use them to your advantage.

One last point. Some people with strong fears or phobias find it difficult to believe that anything will help them. In one study in which over 90 percent of the participants *significantly* reduced their fears, over 60 percent started off believing they would *not* be helped. So even if it is hard to believe that anything will help you, apply yourself to the present treatment program. Give it a chance. Remember that this program has helped many people; don't let your pessimism prevent *you* from working hard and helping yourself.

WHAT TO DO NOW

I have covered a number of points which clarify the nature of fears and phobias, how your program will work, and what you will do to overcome your specific anxieties. I suggest that you put this book aside for now and wait until your first regularly scheduled session before going on to the next chapter. During that session you will read about your relaxation program. Studying the instructions and rules of the program will probably take a whole session. Then, in your second regular meeting, you will begin to teach yourself relaxation skills. Most of you will spend two or three weeks acquiring these skills. After that you will plan your strategy for gradual approach. Depending on how hard you work and how often you hold your sessions, the *entire* program will probably take about eight weeks.

By the way, if you treat this program as an adventure, you may even enjoy the experience. Good luck, and work hard.

4

LEARNING TO RELAX

It is now time for you to learn how to relax. Today, you should spend your entire session studying the instructions and learning all the rules of your program. *Do not actually practice the procedures today.* You will begin doing that *after* you have learned what to do.

LEARNING THE RULES OF YOUR PROGRAM

Learning to relax is a skill; and like any other skill, it takes practice to do it well. That is why many of you will take at least three regularly scheduled sessions to acquire a sense of deep relaxation. Some of you may even spend six sessions or more.

Remember that expecting "immediate results" and trying too hard will only make you tense. So don't be concerned if progress seems slow. As long as you work at the procedures and practice them conscientiously, you should enjoy definite feelings of relaxation by the end of your program.

One of the best ways to identify feelings of relaxation is to alternately tense and relax various muscle groups in your body. This is the basic principle on which your program is based. To illustrate how this works, you can practice a demonstration trial right now. Take your dominant hand (if you're right-handed, use your right hand; if left-handed, use your left hand) and make a loose fist without applying any pressure. Continue to read these instructions. When you come across the word *now* in big capital letters, *slightly* tighten your fist and notice the tension you produce. You'll probably feel tension in your knuckles, in your fingers, and in other parts of your hand. You may also feel tension spreading into the lower part of your arm. Remember not to tense so hard that it hurts. Just make your fist tight enough to feel slight increases in tension.

When you make the fist, hold it for about five to seven seconds. Then, when you see the word *relax* in capital letters, throw away the tension by quickly opening your hand and relaxing the muscles.

All right, get ready by making yourself comfortable. Have your arm resting on the chair you are in and NOW—slightly tighten your fist and hold it. Do you feel tension in your fingers? In your knuckles? Does tension spread to your wrist and forearm? Briefly study the tension in your hand and now RELAX your fist. Rest your hand comfortably on the chair or in your lap and experience some of the tension you purposefully created leave the tense areas. Study the changing sensations.

It doesn't matter if the effects you observe are large or small. It doesn't even matter if your hand still feels a little tense. The purpose of this demonstration was just to illustrate the basic procedural components of relaxation training. *By alternately tens-*

ing and relaxing muscles, you can learn to replace feelings of tension with a comfortable state of relaxation. During the "tension phases" of your program you learn to identify specific points where muscle tension exists for you. For example, when you make a fist you may find that tension builds in your knuckles, in the tips of your fingers, or in your wrist. You may feel tension in the palm of your hand—then again, you may not. Purposefully tensing muscles gives you a chance to study where it is that *your* muscles get tight. Tensing muscles also lets you feel what it is like when tension leaves your body during the "relaxation phases" of your program. As your muscles relax you can contrast the opposing feelings of tension and relaxation. With practice, you will learn to gain control over this process and further extend the feelings of relaxation throughout your muscle groups.

You may be wondering about alternative procedures that people recommend for tension problems. These include yoga, meditation, and hypnosis, to name just a few. One advantage to the muscle relaxation approach in this program is that you learn a skill that you can use in almost *any situation.* Some of the other methods that people use often require the assistance of a professional; and their use is often restricted to quiet settings in which you can meditate undisturbed.

A list of the muscle groups included in your program is provided below. In this list, fifteen individual muscles are listed within four *major groups.* You should read about each of these muscles and see how you most prefer to tense them. Briefly create a slight amount of tension in each muscle as you read down the list. *Don't* confuse this exercise with the actual training program, since you are *not* supposed to alternately tense and relax the muscles. Instead, you are simply identifying the methods of tensing muscles that are best suited to your individual needs.

You will probably find it helpful if you take some notes on page 33. This page will provide a convenient list of the various muscles and how you prefer to tense them.

MAJOR GROUP 1:
THE HANDS AND ARMS

A. Dominant Hand and Forearm: This is the muscle group you just tensed by making a fist and holding it tight.

B. Dominant Biceps: This is the upper-arm muscle that bulges when you "make a muscle" like the "strong man" on the beach. Tense this group by keeping your arm flat on the chair and pushing down with your elbow. If this doesn't work, do like the muscle men and bend your arm at the elbow so your hand faces toward your shoulder. Then apply what is called a "counter-force" by trying to touch your shoulder with your hand while at the same time opposing this movement. Your hand will seem frozen in mid-air by the two opposing forces.

C. Nondominant Hand and Forearm: Just like before, make a fist—but this time use your nondominant hand.

D. Nondominant Biceps: Follow the same procedures described for the dominant biceps.

MAJOR GROUP 2:
THE HEAD, FACE, AND THROAT

A. Forehead: To tense the muscles in your forehead, try lifting your eyebrows high as if you wanted them to touch the top of your head. An alternative method is to frown or "knit your brows."

B. Cheeks and Nose: Squint your eyes and wrinkle your nose. Don't be afraid of making funny faces when you're practicing!

C. Jaws: These muscles can be tensed by clenching your teeth together hard and pulling back the corners of your mouth.

D. Lips and Tongue: With teeth separated, press your lips

**RECORD ON THIS PAGE THE BEST METHOD
FOR CREATING TENSION IN EACH MUSCLE GROUP**

MUSCLE GROUP   METHOD OF TENSING

MAJOR GROUP 1

Dominant hand and forearm _____

Dominant biceps _____

Nondominant hand and forearm _____

Nondominant biceps _____

MAJOR GROUP 2

Forehead _____

Cheeks and nose _____

Jaws _____

Lips and tongue _____

Neck and throat _____

MAJOR GROUP 3

Chest _____

Shoulders and upper back _____

Stomach _____

MAJOR GROUP 4

Thighs and buttocks _____

Calves _____

Feet _____

together and then press your tongue against the roof of your mouth.

E. Neck and Throat: Pull your chin down as if trying to touch it to your chest. Now apply a counterpressure or opposing force to stop your chin. If this method doesn't work, you can press your head back if your chair is tall enough, or if you are sitting up against a wall.

MAJOR GROUP 3:
THE CHEST AND STOMACH

A. Chest: To tense the muscles in your chest, take a deep breath and hold it. Then exhale in an even and smooth manner. Don't breathe out so slowly that you exert effort holding air in; and don't breathe so fast that you push air out. Instead, exhale at whatever rate requires the *least* effort. In this way your muscles can become more fully relaxed. You will see during practice sessions that controlled breathing can increase general levels of relaxation throughout your body.

B. Shoulders and Upper Back: Pull your shoulders up as if they were being held by strings attached to the ceiling. Then arch them back as if trying to touch your shoulder blades together.

C. Stomach: These muscles are most easily tensed by either making your stomach hard, pulling your stomach in and holding it tight, or pushing your stomach out.

MAJOR GROUP 4:
THE LEGS AND FEET

A. Thighs and Buttocks: Tense the muscles in these areas by pressing your heels into the ground and tightening the muscles in your buttocks. An alternative counterforce method involves pressing your knees toward each other while at the same time applying pressure to keep them apart. If neither method produces noticeable tension, try lifting your legs straight out in front of you.

B. Calves: Point your toes up toward your head. Alternatively, point your toes down *away* from your head.

C. Feet: These muscles can easily cramp. So, rather than holding tension for five to seven seconds, use a shorter three-second period. Tense your feet by pointing them slightly down, turning them inward, and curling your toes.

Go over your list several times until you become familiar with each of the muscle groups. It's a good idea to do this now before you rush on to the next set of instructions.

HOW TO PRACTICE TENSING AND RELAXING EACH MUSCLE GROUP

When you begin to actually practice tensing and relaxing the muscle groups in your program, be sure to work on them in their listed order. Thus, start with your hand and arm muscles, then practice your facial muscles, and so on down the list. You can practice these muscles while sitting in a comfortable chair or while lying down. The important point is that you want to be in a comfortable place that is removed from all distractions.

You shouldn't expect to get through all the muscles on your list during your first few sessions. Instead, just do as many groups as you can while following these eight rules:

1. When first practicing a particular group, tense the appropriate muscles for a five to seven-second period. The only exceptions to this rule are your feet and other muscles that may have a tendency to cramp. When practicing these groups, decrease the tension period to about three seconds.

2. You do *not* want to tense your muscles so hard that they hurt. Use the *smallest necessary* amount of tension to identify each distinct point of muscle tightness. One of the most common errors that people make in this type of program is to use too much tension. Be certain you don't do this.

3. After the five-to-seven second tension period, you want to actively reduce tension by quickly releasing your hold on the muscles. Then, for a period of twenty to thirty seconds, spend your time consciously extending feelings of relaxation throughout your muscles. During this period, concentrate on the contrast between tension and relaxation. Remember that some muscle fibers may still be tensed even when you are starting to feel relaxed. Relaxing is an active process of undoing tension, and you want to extend that process as far as possible.

4. Each muscle group should be practiced at least *twice* before proceeding to a new one. If, after two trials, there is no residual tension and your muscles feel relaxed, you can start working with the next muscle group on your list. If tension remains, you should continue to practice the same group for as many as five trials in a single session; then stop and go to the next group.

5. Tensing a muscle can sometimes affect a neighboring group. When you can, try to keep the involvement of adjacent muscles to a minimum. Sometimes, however, this can prove difficult. For example, tensing the arm often leads to a tightening up of the fist as well. There is nothing wrong with this as long as you remember to focus attention *only* on the particular muscle group you are practicing.

6. When you finish all the muscles in a major group, take some time to review them and relax more fully. For instance, when you have finished practicing your hands and arms (Major Group 1), spend a minute or so ex-

tending relaxation further and further. Let yourself experience even greater levels of comfort. After this "review break" you can start the individual muscles in the next major group.

7. Throughout the relaxation phases of the procedure, let yourself enjoy the relaxing effects of exhaling evenly and smoothly. Exhaling is a very relaxing portion of the breathing cycle. It's a good feeling and, with practice, you can learn to take full advantage of it. As you exhale, think to yourself relaxing expressions or words like *calm, peaceful, serene.*

8. Always practice with your eyes closed. This eliminates distractions and lets you focus your full attention on the changing sensations in your muscles. (Naturally, if you are afraid of the dark and don't like to close your eyes, you would not follow this step).

Now, let's review the rules again.

First, practice each muscle group in its listed order by alternately tensing and relaxing the muscle at least twice. If a group remains tense, you can practice it up to five times in a single session. When you have finished all the muscles in a major group, take some time to extend relaxation to deeper and deeper levels. To do this, take advantage of relaxing expressions and the effects of exhaling evenly and smoothly. As you practice, remember to keep your attention focused on just one muscle group at a time.

After your review breaks, continue on to the muscles in the next major group and practice them in the same way. Follow this procedure for thirty to forty minutes during each of your sessions, completing as many of the muscle groups as you can.

To effectively teach yourself relaxation skills you need to know appropriate expressions for tensing and relaxing. In a clinical setting, a therapist would take you through the procedures and tell you at each point what to do. At home, you are your own therapist and you need to "instruct" yourself. A sample set of instructions is given below to illustrate how you might tell yourself what to do. While these instructions have been written for the forehead muscles, similar expressions could be used for any of the muscle groups.

> I'm going to relax my entire body to the best of my ability. I'm settling back now and getting comfortable. I'm ready to begin practicing and I'm going to tighten up my forehead, NOW . . . keep my forehead wrinkled . . . tight . . . experience the tension in my muscles and now . . . RELAX . . . throw away the tightness and do the opposite of tensing . . . relax . . . let go of all the tension and spread the feelings of relaxation all over . . . experience the contrast between tension and relaxation . . . OK, once again, NOW tense my forehead . . . that's right, put tension back into my muscles and again study the tension . . . hold the tension another few seconds and now RELAX again . . . enjoy the contrast . . . let me see how far I can extend the process . . . letting the relaxation spread over my forehead . . . relaxing . . . relaxing.

Try reading the above example again. Practice creating an initial sense of tension as you read along. Then experience how the relaxation instructions can help create a lazy, calm feeling of restfullnes.

Professionals tend to use several standard phrases during relaxation training. Expressions that can be used during the *relaxation* phases of your program include:

> Note how I feel as relaxation takes place . . .
>
> More and more relaxed, more than ever before . . .
>
> Completely relaxed, warm and relaxed . . .
>
> Feel the relaxation and warmth flow through my muscles . .
>
> Throw away the tension . . .
>
> Notice the difference between tension and relaxation . . .
>
> Feel the relaxation throughout my muscles . . .

Relax and smooth out the muscles . . .

Relax to the best of my ability. . . .

Feel calm, rested . . .

Focus on the contrast between tension and relaxation . . .

Continue letting go . . . relax . . . relax . . .

Let the tension dissolve away . . .

Expressions for the *tension* phases of your training program are generally less varied; the ones listed below should prove helpful.

Feel the muscles pull . . . hold it . . .

Tighten my muscles . . .

Pay attention to these muscles . . . identify the tension . . .

Study (attend to) the tension . . .

Notice where the tightness is for me . . .

Put tension into my muscles . . .

The expressions for tensing and relaxing muscles can be used interchangeably with any individual group. Note that during practice sessions you will only say instructional phrases to yourself *SILENTLY*. If you actually said the instructions out loud, you would exert effort in the muscles of your mouth and jaw, and that would interfere with deep relaxation.

HOW TO SCHEDULE YOUR SESSIONS

You have already set up for yourself at least two regular appointment times each week. Starting with your *next* regular meeting, you can begin working on the muscle groups in your program. Start with the muscles in your dominant hand, then go on to your arm, and continue down your list practicing each muscle in its proper order. Don't expect to get much further than your facial muscles during the first session. This is because you are likely to experience tension in some muscles and these groups will be practiced as many as five times.

All sessions after the first one should start at the beginning of your muscle list. For example, if you complete the muscles of the hands, arms, and face during the first session, your second session will still start with the hands. This does *not* mean that you'll never complete all the muscles on your list. As you get better at relaxing muscles in only two trials, you will learn to move rapidly from one group to the next. In that way you will eventually complete every group in a single session.

When therapists in a clinic use relaxation training, they tell their patients to practice at home twice a day for 10 to 15 minutes at a time. Since regularly scheduled sessions are equivalent to meeting with a therapist, it is important that you also "practice at home" for short periods. Some convenient times for holding daily practice sessions are when you first wake up in the morning, between appointments during the day, and when you are getting ready for bed.

Do *not* use your daily practice sessions to start *new* muscle groups. Instead, use these sessions to work on muscles *previously* practiced in your regular sessions. For example, if just the muscles in Major Group 1 were completed during your first session, you would only practice these muscles on a daily basis. This practice would improve your skills so that you could progress more quickly to new muscle groups during your second session.

POSSIBLE PROBLEMS

In addition to learning the program's rules, you want to be aware of difficulties that people sometimes experience. The major problems encountered by professionals when they train clients are: (a) distractions in the environment; (b) distracting behaviors such as laughing, sneezing, coughing, and fidgeting; (c) unpleasant sensations and muscle cramps that may accompany relaxation; and, (d) intrusive thoughts that are unpleasant or arousing. For each of these potential problems there are things you can do.

DISTRACTIONS

It goes without saying that you want to keep distractions to a minimum by finding a private and comfortable place to hold your sessions. Also keep down distracting behaviors by closely monitoring yourself and refraining from unnecessary movements. If you have a cold and find yourself coughing or sneezing, it might be a good idea to postpone a session. Use your judgment to arrange the environment so distracting factors are kept to a minimum.

UNPLEASANT SENSATIONS

Sensations which some people initially find uncomfortable or strange can accompany feelings of relaxation. These may include tingling or floating sensations, dizzy feelings in your head, and small muscle spasms or jerks. If it's any comfort for you to know, these reactions are not unusual. They can even be signals that you are becoming more relaxed. If you do feel sensations that initially seem uncomfortable, don't make the mistake of moving your muscles around in an attempt to adjust them. You may think this makes your muscles feel better, but all you are really doing is exerting effort and preventing yourself from becoming relaxed. If odd sensations occur, simply remain still; exert no effort. Notice how the sensations will lessen in their intensity and blend into more comfortable feelings of relaxation. Naturally, small muscle spasms and tingling sensations are to be distinguished from uncomfortable muscle cramps. If the latter occur, it is important to reduce the time interval for tensing muscles or to apply less force when making the muscles tense.

PHYSICAL TENSION

A few people who practice this program find the procedures physically arousing rather than relaxing. If you have this reaction, *decrease* the extent to which you actually tense your muscles during the tension phases of the program. Do this by gradually and slowly tightening a muscle group until you feel the *slightest noticeable* increase in muscle tension. Then stop, don't tense up any more, and study that very small amount of tension. It will be enough to help you identify tension points relevant to you.

DISTURBING THOUGHTS

It is not uncommon for people to report anxiety producing or arousing thoughts that disrupt their feelings of relaxation. Generally, the distracting influence of these thoughts will lessen with time. One approach to actively counteract disruptive thoughts is to purposefully call to mind a pleasant image. For example, if you can't stop thinking about a particular incident that makes you tense, try concentrating on a different and more relaxing scene. You can imagine yourself sitting under a tree on a beautiful spring day. Let this scene capture your full attention by adding details and making it as real as possible.

FEELING SLEEPY

One last problem needs to be mentioned. If you find yourself dozing off, you can be sure your efforts to relax have been successful. Unfortunately, once you are asleep, you can no longer practice. And effectively developing relaxation skills does require continued effort and hard work. So try to stay awake!

BE MENTALLY RELAXED

Up to now you have focused your attention on the physical side of relaxation. You have learned about various muscle groups and the appropriate methods for tensing and relaxing them. *Just as important as physical relaxation is your ability to feel mentally relaxed.* You can accomplish this by thinking to yourself a word like "relax", "calm," or "serene" while breathing in a smooth and even manner. Think about the word or some other calming statement as you breathe out, and notice how exhaling is the most relaxing part of the breathing cycle.

Throughout your program remember these two tricks: pleasant self-instructions and controlled breathing. These procedures are the key to feeling mentally relaxed. They can help you feel relaxed even when it is difficult to eliminate physical tension from your muscles.

GETTING READY TO BEGIN

You have covered a lot of new material today. It may be a good idea to spend part of your next session going over it again. Before you actually practice the procedures, be sure you understand what muscle groups are involved, the rules for tensing and relaxing, the kinds of instructions to give yourself, how to schedule sessions, and common problems you may encounter.

To test your mastery of this material, see if you can correctly answer the following questions. *After* you have circled what you think are the correct answers, check the Answer Key on the bottom of p. 46.

QUIZ

1. Progressive relaxation is learned by: (*a*) trying hard to relax on your own; (*b*) alternately tensing and relaxing different muscle groups; (*c*) listening to relaxing records and thinking pleasant thoughts; (*d*) meditating about a happy thought for half-hour periods.
2. If you experience muscle cramps while tensing a muscle group, you should: (*a*) apply less force when making the muscles tight; (*b*) reduce the time interval used for tensing the group; (*c*) stop practicing and go on to the next group; (*d*) both (*a*) and (*b*) are correct, but (*c*) is wrong.
3. Intrusive thoughts which distract you from relaxing will probably go away on their own, but if you want, you can reduce this problem by: (*a*) purposefully thinking of pleasant scenes; (*b*) listening to music to distract you from these thoughts; (*c*) holding a conversation with someone in the room to keep your mind off things; (*d*) unfortunately, there isn't anything you can do to help this problem.
4. During the tension phases of your program be sure to: (*a*) make your muscles real tight so you feel them straining; (*b*) let the tension spread through as much of your body as possible; (*c*) focus on only one muscle group at a time and create small identifiable increases in tension; (*d*) keep your eyes open so you can watch the muscles straining.
5. Imagine that you have successfully practiced the muscles in Major Groups 1, 2, and 3 and you are now ready to begin your fourth regular session. With which indivi-

dual muscle group would you start? (*a*) your dominant hand; (*b*) your forehead; (*c*) your chest; (*d*) your thighs.

6. Daily practice sessions can help you: (*a*) start new muscle groups; (*b*) build up your muscle strength by really tensing each group; (*c*) get better at muscles you already practiced in the regular meetings; (*d*) both (*a*) and (*b*) are true.

Go ahead now and check the Answer Key on p. 46. If you miss any question, you should study again the relevant instructional sections. Once you have mastered all the information, you can begin working on the listed muscle groups. If your progress is rapid, you may experience little difficulty working through all the groups in only two or three sessions. But finishing your program this quickly would be unusual. Most of you will spend four to six regularly scheduled sessions learning to adequately relax. Gradual progress is not uncommon and should not cause concern. Regardless of the number of sessions it takes to learn relaxation skills, you should be able to achieve success in the end.

What you practice on a particular day depends, of course, on your progress in each session. During regular sessions, practice the various groups in their listed order for thirty to forty minutes. Use daily practice sessions to work on especially difficult groups and to increase your general skills. To help you schedule sessions and keep track of your progress, you should use the Log Sheets on pp. 47-48.

There is one more thing to remember as you get ready to begin. The start of your relaxation program is only a *first* step toward your final goal. Some people wonder why they are supposed to sit in a chair and alternately tense and relax various muscle groups. After all, it isn't easy to see how this will eliminate fears and tensions in real life! Such doubts are understandable, but keep in mind that you are just starting your treatment program. You are learning the beginning or basic skills. Once the foundations of your program are established, you will work on the next section of instructions and apply what you have learned to real-life situations. But first, you need to work on the individual muscles. So start to practice during your next regularly scheduled session, work hard, and you will have success.

Answer Key:

1. (*b*)
2. (*d*)
3. (*a*)
4. (*c*)
5. (*a*)
6. (*c*).

LOG SHEET
FOR BASIC RELAXATION PROGRAM

General Instructions: Find a comfortable place to hold your sessions. (Most people prefer to practice in a large stuffed chair that offers support for their neck.) Whatever place you choose, be sure it will be free from distractions. It should afford you total privacy.

Remember to tense muscles for 5-7 seconds, relax them for 20-30 seconds. Only tense your muscles enough so you can identify points of tension relevant for you. Don't overtense!

If you become uncertain of the procedures, go back and read the relevant instructional sections in your program.

DATE OF SESSION	TYPE OF SESSION	WHAT WAS PRACTICED
Jan. 10	First Regular	Started with dominant hand and worked through facial muscles to mouth.
Jan. 11	Daily Practice	Mostly worked on forehead and eyes.
Jan. 12	Daily Practice	Forehead and eyes getting easier to relax.
Jan. 13	Daily Practice	Reviewed hands and arms, forehead and eyes now easy.
Jan. 14	Second Regular	Started with dominant hand and this time got through to my stomach muscles—some difficulty relaxing shoulders.
Jan. 15	Daily Practice	Focused on relaxing shoulders.

EXAMPLE—EXAMPLE—EXAMPLE—EXAMPLE

| DATE OF | TYPE | WHAT WAS |
SESSION	OF SESSION	PRACTICED

STOP!

Do not continue to the next section of instructions until you can relax all the muscles on your list. Be sure to keep a record of your sessions on the Log Sheets.

INCREASING YOUR EFFICIENCY

Up to now you have practiced a series of procedures that would be difficult to use in real life. It is hard to imagine any situation where you would want to sit down for twenty minutes to alternately tense and relax fifteen individual muscle groups! The next few pages teach you how to relax more efficiently in real-life situations. This section will be helpful *only* if you have first learned to successfully relax each of the individual muscles in your program. Do not begin this section until you have honestly completed the previous exercises.

The best way to approach this set of instructions is to spend today's session reading about the various exercises. You can then start to work on the procedures during your next regularly scheduled session or during your short daily practice sessions. A new set of Log Sheets is provided at the end of these instructions (pp. 55-56) to help you record your progress.

COMBINING MUSCLE GROUPS

The first step in improving your relaxation skills is to "combine" the muscles in each major group. This will dramatically shorten the time it takes to get your *entire* body relaxed. In your next session, start with Major Group 1 and simultaneously tense both fists and both biceps for the usual five-to-seven-second period. Then, all together, release your hold on these muscles and let yourself become relaxed all over. Spend a good thirty to sixty seconds letting relaxation spread throughout the muscles in your hands and arms. After this period, practice for a second time the muscles in Major Group 1.

People often feel residual muscle tension when they first combine groups. When this happens, all you need to do is practice in the usual way those muscles that still feel tense. For example, when combining the muscles in Major Group 1, your left biceps may remain tense during and after the relaxation periods. In that case, you would pay individual attention to your left biceps and practice them alone. When this part of your arm felt fully relaxed, you could go back to tensing and relaxing the entire major group.

It will probably take at least one full session to learn how to combine muscles in each of the four major groups. Use your practice sessions after that to further learn this efficient way to relax.

ELIMINATING THE TENSION PHASES OF YOUR PROGRAM

After you have learned to combine individual muscle groups, you can begin to "fade out" the tension phases of your program. Do this by gradually reducing the extent to which you purposefully tense your muscles. Within a few practice sessions, you won't be tensing at all.

People are glad when they can drop the obvious and sometimes awkward tension exercises. Originally these exercises were needed to help you learn specific points where tension develops in your body. Now you know where to check for tension so it should only be necessary to tighten muscles when you are out of practice and need a reminder.

In addition to practicing at home, you can begin to think about tension in real-life settings. Several times a day, try to check relevant tension points and see if your muscles are tight. You can do this in just about any setting since you won't actually tense your muscle groups. For example, you might be sitting with friends enjoying a cup of coffee. Just for the fun of it, you could mentally check over the various tension points in your body—your friends won't even know you're doing this. With practice you will become increasingly skillful at spot-checking relevant tension points throughout your body. It won't be necessary to tense these points since you will have learned where they are and what they feel like.

CUE WORDS AND BREATHING

You may have already developed the habit of saying to yourself words like *calm, relax,* or *serene* during the relaxation phases of your program. You may have also learned to focus on the relaxing effects of exhaling smoothly and evenly. Now you want to begin using these two procedures to greater advantage. You can do this by getting all your muscles fully relaxed and then reviewing each individual group in the following manner. Think of your dominant hand while breathing in and then out. The next time you inhale and exhale, shift the focus of your attention to your dominant biceps. During the next breathing cycle concentrate on your nondominant hand. Continue to shift your attention *in coordination* with your breathing until you have reviewed the fifteen muscle groups on your original list.

After you have gone through the entire list, try practicing the procedure once again while adding one more step. This time whenever you exhale, say to yourself one of the relaxing "cue words" you like to use. Thus, you would first think of your dominant hand as you inhaled. Then, when you exhaled, you would keep your attention on your hand while thinking "calm," "serene," or "relax" or whatever word you preferred.

Once you are familiar with the rhythm of breathing and relaxing, you can extend the use of the cue word to your combined muscle groups. Start with Major Group 1 and focus your attention on each of your relevant tension points. Keep your attention on these points as you breath in and out, in and out. Each time you exhale, think of your cue word and let it carry you into deeper levels of relaxation. After two breathing cycles, switch your attention to the next major group and continue to follow the same procedure. Since there are only four major groups, you will be learning to review your muscles and feel fully relaxed in only eight breaths.

You can start to employ these procedures in each of your daily sessions. In this way, your cue word will become strongly associated with feelings of deep relaxation. The next section teaches you how to apply this word in real-life situations.

PUTTING IT ALL TOGETHER

This is the final part of your relaxation program. Before you begin working on this section be sure you can:

1. Relax individual muscle groups
2. Relax combined muscles in the four major groups
3. Spot-check relevant tension points without purposefully tensing your muscles
4. Pair a cue word with exhaling evenly and smoothly

Once you have developed these skills you will be ready to put them all together so you can relax quickly and efficiently. During your *daily practice sessions* you will follow these procedures. Start by getting comfortable in *any* chair in your house. Then begin to relax your body by focusing on the combined muscles in your four major groups. It should only be necessary to tense a particular group if you have trouble getting it relaxed. Throughout your sessions be sure to remain aware of the relaxing effects of exhaling evenly. Use your cue word to coordinate your breathing and relaxation efforts.

Because this procedure is so easy, you can try it several times a day. As you become better at rapidly relaxing at home, begin to extend your skills to other settings. Simply spot-check yourself whenever you want. If you notice that your muscles are unnecessarily tense, do the following: focus your attention on the points you want to relax; become aware of your breathing; and think to yourself your cue word each time you exhale. This three-step procedure

1. Identify tension, 2. Regulate breathing, and 3. Use cue words and exhale

can be used in most any situation to extend feelings of relaxation throughout your body.

There is one additional skill you will want to spend some time developing. Even in settings where you must exert some muscle effort it is often possible to use your energy more efficiently. For example, the next time you are driving, take a minute to think about your muscles. Obviously you will be exerting effort in your arms and in your feet. But is it possible that your shoulders are unnecessarily tense? Can you get your left foot to feel fully relaxed when it isn't being used? Those of you who don't drive can think of other situations where you may not use your muscles as efficiently as possible. The basic point is that you can decrease the amount of energy that is needlessly spent during the day by concentrating on only those muscles you really need to use.

A FINAL POINT

When you have mastered all of the previous exercises your level of relaxation skills will help reduce many everyday tensions; but your skills will *not* eliminate strong fears and phobias. It takes more work to do that. So for the time being, do *not* go out and confront your fears thinking you can relax them away. It won't be until *after* the next chapter (Step 3 of your program) that you will begin the actual process of overcoming your fear or phobia. Be patient and remember to take things one step at a time.

Although there is certainly more work to be done, you have almost completed the first step in your treatment. If you were at a clinic your therapist would pause to mention the significance of your accomplishment. Since you are your own therapist, take some time before the next chapter to congratulate yourself. You can now relax your muscles and use them more efficiently.

LOG SHEET
FOR INCREASING YOUR EFFICIENCY

General Instructions: Follow the procedural steps as they are shown in the examples below. Whenever necessary, you can spend more than one session on a particular exercise before going on to the next step.

DATE OF SESSION	TYPE OF SESSION	WHAT WAS PRACTICED
Jan. 26	Regular	Spent entire session learning to combine muscle groups—had some difficulty with facial muscles.
Jan. 27-Jan. 29	Daily Practice	Combined groups—concentrated on facial muscles—getting easier.
Jan. 30	Regular	Began to fade out tension phases of program—also used controlled breathing and cue words.
Jan. 30-Feb. 1	Daily Practice	Relaxed combined muscle groups with only slight tension. I have been spot-checking myself three times a day.
Feb. 2	Regular	Started to work on Chapter 5. I no longer use the regular meetings to work on the relaxation program.
Feb. 3	Daily Practice	I will continue daily practice sessions to gain better control over muscle tension in everyday situations.

EXAMPLE—EXAMPLE—EXAMPLE—EXAMPLE

DATE OF SESSION	TYPE OF SESSION	WHAT WAS PRACTICED

5

PLANNING YOUR STRATEGY FOR APPROACH

At this point in the program some people get impatient and want to "test" themselves in real-life situations. A woman afraid of spiders approaches a small one in the kitchen and tries to relax away her tension. A car phobic decides to get into the car and drive around the neighborhood. I strongly recommend that you *avoid* doing this, since you will only set yourself up for possible failure and disappointment. You may be ready to *plan* your strategy for approach, but you are *not* ready to actually do things in real life. Try to be patient, relax, and follow the procedures in this book one step at a time.

Planning your strategy for gradual approach takes less time than did training in relaxation skills. In fact, most of you will spend only two regularly scheduled sessions on this part of the program. Don't let this shorter amount of time mislead you into thinking this section is less important. If anything, just the opposite is true: your approach strategy is *critical* to a successful program. Follow the procedures in this chapter *carefully* and take your work seriously.

Now that I have discussed what you should and should not do, let's see how a successful strategy for approach is planned. The first thing to consider is what it is that you actually fear. This is an important issue since you don't want to spend time approaching the wrong thing.

As it turns out, the question "What are you afraid of?" is not as simple to answer as you might think. For example, if you told me you were afraid of airplane travel, I still wouldn't know what really bothered you. Some people are made anxious by the cramped quarters of an airplane's cabin; so their fear is of closed-in places. Other people are upset when they look out the plane's windows and see the height at which they are flying. Still others are anxious only during takeoff and landing when accidents may be more likely.

In a similar way, I wouldn't really know what you feared if you said "job interviews." You might be afraid of speaking in public. Or perhaps you get anxious when speaking to males and you think a male will conduct your interview. There are a variety of other factors in an interview situation, any one of which could be the basis of your fear. You could even be afraid because you think an interview would go well and you would get a job—the real thing you fear is the new job responsibilities you would then have to cope with!

These examples illustrate how feared objects or situations have many aspects or *dimensions* to them. It is one thing to say you are afraid of airplanes, job interviews, doctors, spiders, or snakes; specifying exactly what makes you anxious is a more complicated matter. Yet this more complicated issue is one with which you need to be concerned. If you were fearful of interviews because speaking in public made you anxious, you would want to plan an approach strategy that increased involvement in social situations and public speaking. On the other hand, if you feared interviews because getting a job meant increased responsibilities, your strategy for approach would be entirely different.

The first step in planning your strategy for approach

requires you to carefully define or *assess* the dimensions of *your* fear. In that way the important characteristics of the objects or situations that upset you can be clearly identified. It will then be possible to plan an approach strategy that is relevant to your particular fear.

ASSESSING THE DIMENSIONS OF YOUR FEAR

It isn't difficult to assess the specific characteristics of a fear or phobia. First, you need to get a pen or pencil. Then take a look at the Assessment Sheet on p. 61. Notice that you are asked first (item 1) to provide a general label for the thing you fear. In this space you should write "doctors," "airplanes," "insects," "public speaking," or whatever general heading you have always used to characterize your fear. Then, below your general heading, in item 2, list all the different characteristics of the feared object or situation that are most relevant to you. For example, under fear of doctors one could list things like "blood," "needles," "nurses," "authority figures," "death," "answering questions," "being naked," and so on. A person afraid of snakes might be concerned about the way snakes move, how they attack or bite people, or how they catch you by surprise. People afraid of elevators might be anxious about cramped quarters, being alone, feeling a sense of falling, or being high up.

Try to list as many *relevant* characteristics as you can. Some of you will only have one or two important points; but if you want, you can list as many as ten. Once you have completed your list, it is possible to "rank-order" each characteristic in terms of its importance to you. For example, you might be afraid of elevators and notice that your fear increases the higher you go, but doesn't change in relation to the number of people in the elevator. In that case, height is more important for you than is being alone or in crowded spaces. If you are afraid of snakes and your anxiety is affected by their size, but not so much by how fast they move, then the shape and size of snakes are clearly more relevant to your fear than movement.

When you have decided what specific feature of the feared object or situation is most important to you, place a "1" next to that listing under "Rank." Then think of the second most important characteristic and place a "2" next to it. In a similar way, you can decide on the relative importance of each characteristic listed on the Assessment Sheet.

After you have ranked the relevant dimensions of your feared object or situation, proceed to the next step of your assessment (item 3). During the next five to ten minutes, try to think of three or four situations in which you have been confronted by the object or situation you fear. Recent experiences are usually best. Recall the situations as clearly as you can, and then jot down some notes on your assessment sheet to remind you of what happened.

When your past situations are down on paper, go back and look at the important characteristics you listed in item 2. Check out your rank-orderings against the situations and see if the elements you thought were important really did influence your reactions. If the situations bring to mind other specific factors relevant to your fear, you can make the appropriate changes in your list of important characteristics. Don't be surprised if you need to do this. I worked with a person who was socially anxious in all group situations—or at least that's what he said. When we reviewed past situations in which he had been upset, the distressing factor turned out to be the presence of females; the number of people present was not really that important.

The next step in this assessment is to consider your *reactions* in past situations (item 4). Write down on the Assessment Sheet the things you said to yourself when you were feeling upset. A few examples of self-statements people with fears often make are: "I feel faint"; "I'm so afraid"; "What will I do?"; "Oh, my God, I think I'm going to die." Whatever you have typically said to yourself when upset should be noted on the Assessment Sheet under "Self-report."

ASSESSMENT SHEET

1. Feared object or situation: _____
2. Important Characteristics:

	Rank			Rank
1_____	____	6_____		____
2_____	____	7_____		____
3_____	____	8_____		____
4_____	____	9_____		____
5_____	____	10_____		____

3. Past Experiences: (if necessary continue your descriptions on the back of this page)

4. Your Reactions:
   Self-report (saying):

   Overt behavior (acting):

   Physical (feeling):

5. General Fear Rating: Indicate how anxious you get when you have contact with the object or situation you fear.

0	1	2	3	4	5	6	7	8	9	10

Truly Not Upset   Moderately Upset   As Upset as I Could Ever Be

What you actually ended up doing should be noted under "Overt behavior." Did you freeze in your tracks and start shaking? Did you scream and run? Did you try to remain calm and confront your fears? Whatever you recall doing in past situations should be recorded on the Assessment Sheet.

Finally, there were probably things you *felt* in addition to what you *said* and *did*. Your stomach may have been tight; you may have perspired; your heart may have beaten fast; or you may have become light-headed and faint. Recall the physical reactions you tend to have when confronted by the thing you fear and note them under "Physical."

Your Assessment Sheet should now contain the following information:

1. A general heading to characterize your fear
2. Those characteristics or dimensions of the thing you fear that are particularly upsetting to you, rank-ordered according to their intensity
3. A description of past situations in which you were afraid
4. A listing of how you react when you get anxious

As a last step in your fear assessment, complete item 5 on your sheet by rating your general level of anxiety when you have contact with the object or situation you fear. Simply circle whatever number best represents your current feelings toward the thing you fear. The higher your number is (further to the right), the more it indicates you are afraid and distressed. The lower your number (further to the left), the less afraid you are. At the end of your program you will be able to respond to this question again. It will be fun to see how large a change has occurred in your answer.

By the way, if thinking about those past situations has created a little anxiety, it would be a good idea to spend several minutes getting comfortable again. Take some even breaths and let yourself relax away the tension. Then move on to the next Section of instruction.

PLANNING YOUR STRATEGY

You may have learned some surprising things during the assessment of your fear reactions. What always seemed like a fear of elevators may have turned out to be a concern over heights. Perhaps your fear of insects primarily relates to ants and other crawling bugs, while flying insects don't really bother you at all. Someone may fear driving a car because of the places he goes, not because of driving per se. Whether or not you learned something new, you have clearly identified the relevant dimensions of your fear. *Your job now is to plan a strategy for approach that will allow you to gradually and systematically confront the specific things that upset you.* Planning this strategy requires a series of scenes or situations involving the object or situation you fear. The scenes will be ordered so as to start off with the least fearful, and gradually build up to the most fearful. In this way, your scenes will be arranged in a hierarchical fashion, each scene building on the one before it. Accordingly, we can speak of an *anxiety hierarchy*, or a list of situations that bring you into increasingly closer contact with the thing you fear.

Some people balk at this point in their program and say they can't construct an anxiety hierarchy. On the one hand, this is an understandable reaction. After all, you are going to list a series of scenes that make you anxious and that you actually *cannot* confront. But remember, at the moment you aren't supposed to *do* any of the things you are now thinking about—you are only *planning* your strategy. When you start practicing scenes in the next chapter, you will follow a specific set of rules that prevent you from becoming too uncomfortable. So relax, and don't worry as you work at the present exercises.

It may help at this point to acquire a general overview of the task that lies ahead. You already know that planning your strategy for approach involves the *construction of an anxiety hierarchy that will permit increasingly close contact with the relevant dimensions of your fear.* To see more clearly what this means, carefully study the ten sample hierarchies on pp. 68-81, which cover the following fears: driving cars; flying in airplanes; the dark; heights; dental or medical procedures; public speaking; job interviews; social dating; spiders; and snakes. It should be noted that these examples do *not* represent completed hierarchies, but merely illustrate the basic skeleton of a hierarchy. This basic skeleton involves the specific *overt behaviors* that will be involved in your strategy for approach. A consideration of what you feel and say (in addition to what you do) is not included until later. Also not included are certain details that will be discussed later in this chapter. For the time being, you simply want to see the kinds of behaviors people can include when they plan their strategy for approach.

You may be tempted to only study the hierarchy that appears most relevant to your fear. But the general headings do not tell you if the *specific* dimensions of a hierarchy are relevant to you. In addition, every example demonstrates certain important points, and useful comments are noted at the bottom of each page. So spend some time studying *all* the examples. This will help you get an idea of the different strategies people use to gradually approach their feared object or situation.

There is even good reason to argue that the hierarchy most relevant to your fear should be studied *last.* If you were to look at it immediately, you would run the risk of exaggerating your own feelings of anxiety. People with fears and phobias tend to think they are unique, and they are frequently embarrassed by their problems. Rushing to look at a "relevant" hierarchy might only reinforce these tendencies.

I have worked with many clients who tell me something about their fears and then ask, "Isn't that silly?" or "Aren't I weird?" When these people learn that others have just as severe fears, they start to see their own problem in a more objective and broader perspective. A person who pretends his stomach hurts to avoid swimming in pools doesn't feel so "weird" after learning that some people won't walk in their own back yards for fear of snakes. Of course, a person who won't walk in his own back yard doesn't feel unusual either, after learning that some people will fake stomachaches to avoid swimming! In a similar vein, there are thousands of people each with a different fear that needlessly embarrasses them. Studying hierarchies that are *not* related to your anxieties can help you see this point more clearly.

As you study the examples there are a few things to notice. First, each of the hierachies are arranged so as to start with the "least fearful" and gradually build up to the "most fearful" scene. Second, the hierarchies contain as few as nine and as many as twenty scenes. The number of scenes needed for your hierarchy will depend on your own special circumstances. If you have a minor fear that can be quickly eliminated, then eight or ten scenes may be sufficient to cover the full range of your anxiety reactions. Alternatively, you may have an exceedingly strong phobia, in which case more scenes will be needed to gradually approach your final goal. If the sample hierarchies seem to approach the feared object or situation too fast, don't be alarmed. You can always include additional scenes in your hierarchy to permit a more gradual approach.

A third point to notice as you study the sample hierarchies is that some of the scenes are *imagined* and never actually practiced, while other scenes involve *real-life* experiences. In general, you will want to practice real-life situations whenever they can be arranged and adequately controlled. Although imagined scenes are useful, practice in real life helps you feel comfortable in the actual settings that bother you. Thus, approaches based on real-life situations are more direct and to the point.

When practice in real-life situations is not possible, imagined scenes have to be used. In addition, imagined scenes are actually preferred when (1) real-life situations are impossible to gradually approach or (2) real-life situations are difficult to terminate. You will see these two conditions illustrated in the sample hierarchy on fear of flying in airplanes. It clearly would be difficult to approach a commercial jet while it was actually taxiing on the runway or waiting for takeoff. It would also be impossible to (safely) terminate a plane flight once it had begun. Accordingly, people afraid of airplanes will want to spend a good deal of time practicing imagined scenes.

During the 1950s and early 1960s, therapists almost entirely relied on imagined scenes. One of the major reasons for this was convenience. If you were afraid of snakes, it would have taken time for you and your therapist to drive to a pet store and look at real animals. It would also have been inconvenient for your therapist to bring a snake into the office. Fortunately, imagined scenes are not only convenient and easy to use, they are also clinically effective. Therapists have found that when patients relax to imagined scenes they also become more comfortable in difficult real-life situations. Thus, imagined scenes provide a very useful *transition* to natural settings.

The types of scenes you choose for your hierarchy will depend on your own special circumstances; but you needn't be concerned with making any decisions now. For the time being, you only need to be aware of the alternatives that will be available to you later in your program.

You will notice that, in the sample hierarchies, friends and relatives are sometimes included in the scenes. Such people can provide support and reduce your anxiety in difficult settings. Your friends and relatives may be especially helpful if you are fearful about doing things in front of strangers. The sample hierarchy on fear of public speaking demonstrates how you can first run through upsetting situations in the presence of friends and relatives; then you can move on to more difficult situations with strangers.

Friends and relatives can also serve as *models*—people who demonstrate for you how something is done. Useful examples of modeled situations can be found in the sample hierarchies on dental, car, and spider phobias.

There is just one caution regarding modeled situations and the inclusion of friends or relatives. Be certain that any person who participates in your program will not pressure you into doing more than you have planned. Your friend or relative should clearly understand that *you* are the person in charge of treatment and that your treatment requires a careful, gradual approach. They are there to help you, but not to give advice nor to demand instant change.

Keep the above points in mind as you study the sample hierarchies and see how creative strategies for overcoming fears and phobias can be planned. After you have studied these examples, you will be in a better position to design *your* strategy for approach.

SAMPLE HIERARCHY FOR FEAR
OF DRIVING CARS

1. I sit in the passenger seat of my car while it is parked in my driveway. The engine is not running.

2. I sit in the driver's seat of the car while it is parked in my driveway. This time the engine is running.

3. I go for a short drive in the car. I am sitting in the back seat and my friend is driving.

4. I go for a short drive in my car. I am sitting in the front passenger seat and my friend is driving.

5. I drive my car down the driveway and back up to the garage. I am alone in the car.

6. I drive the car down the block and return home. My friend is with me and is sitting in the front passenger seat.

7. I drive the car down the block and return home. My friend is with me and is sitting in the back seat.

8. I drive the car down the block and return home. My friend is following behind me in a separate car.

9. With my friend following behind me, I drive for 10 minutes around my neighborhood.

10. Without my friend following me, I drive for 5 minutes around my neighborhood.
11. Without my friend following me, I drive for 10 minutes around my neighborhood.
12. With my friend driving, I go downtown and return home.
13. I drive downtown and return home. My friend follows behind me in another car.
14. I drive downtown and return home. This time my friend only follows me downtown. I drive home alone.
15. I drive downtown and return home totally on my own.

Comments: Notice how this hierarchy makes use of a friend to provide support and *model* appropriate performance in difficult situations. The friend is gradually *phased out* of each new situation. You will also notice that this person's anxiety is affected by the seating arrangements in the car.

SAMPLE HIERARCHY FOR FEAR OF FLYING IN AIRPLANES

1. I look at an advertisement for an airplane flight to Europe.
2. I look at color pictures of airplanes.
3. I visit an airport and look at the planes. While I am there I see a friend or relative board a plane to go on vacation.
4. I call an airline and practice getting flight information.
5. I arrange with a local pilot to visit the airport and see a small private plane.
6. I visit the airport and see the planes. I sit inside the pilot's small plane while the engine is started. There is no attempt to fly the plane. I just get comfortable sitting in the cabin.
7. I imagine myself on a regular jet plane getting ready for

takeoff. The details for this and the remaining scenes I imagine are provided by a friend or relative.

8. I imagine myself on a jet while it is in flight. I am with several friends or relatives.

9. I imagine myself on a jet while it is in flight. I am by myself.

10. I imagine myself on a jet while it is in flight. I am by myself and the ride is somewhat bumpy.

11. I imagine myself on a jet by myself and the plane is landing.

12. I take a short plane flight with a friend or relative.

Comments: Flying in a plane presents a special problem since the situation cannot be fully controlled. Once you have taken off you need to stay there until you land. For this reason, a person afraid of airplanes should spend time getting completely comfortable with imagined scenes. To do this properly a person would have to acquire as much information as possible to know what a plane flight is really like. In addition to asking friends or relatives who fly, it may help to see movies in which there are scenes of an airplane in flight.

If you are afraid of airplanes, you may want to check with the local airlines to see if you can walk through a plane while it is on the ground. Getting comfortable in a plane's cabin may be of tremendous help.

SAMPLE HIERARCHY FOR FEAR
OF THE DARK

1. I am in a room with a friend and the lighting is fairly dim.

2. My friend and I light two candles and I turn off all the electric lights.

3. My friend and I are in the room together and I blow out one of the candles.

4. My friend and I are in the room together. My friend blows out the remaining candle and we talk to each other while the room is dark. After 5 seconds my friend turns on an electric light.

5. My friend and I are in the room with one candle burning. My friend blows out the candle and we talk to each other while it remains dark. After 20 seconds we turn on a light.

6. My friend and I repeat scene 5, but this time we don't talk.

7. My friend and I repeat scene 6, but this time we wait a full minute before turning on the light.

8. My friend and I repeat scene 7, but this time we wait 5 minutes before turning on the light.

9. I am alone in the room and the electric lighting is dim.

10. I am alone in the room and there are only two candles lit.

11. I am alone in the room and there is only one candle lit.

12. I am alone in the room and there is only one candle lit. I call my friend on the phone, blow out the candle, and talk for a couple of minutes. Then I turn on the electric light and finish my phone conversation.

13. I am alone in the room and there is one candle lit. I blow it out and wait 5 seconds before I turn on the electric light.

14. I repeat step 13, but this time I wait 20 seconds.

15. I repeat step 13, but this time I wait a full minute.

16. I repeat step 13, but this time I wait 5 full minutes.

Comments: If you have a rheostat in your house (a device that gradually dims the lighting in a room), you can use this to your advantage. Naturally the number of steps you include in your hierarchy will depend on how anxious you feel and how gradually you need to approach your final goal.

SAMPLE HIERARCHY FOR FEAR
OF HEIGHTS

1. I stand on a chair in my house.
2. I stand on a table in my house.
3. I look out a closed window from the 2nd story of a downtown building.
4. I look out a closed window from the 4th story of a downtown building.
5. I look out an open window from the 4th story.
6. I approach an open doorway leading onto a fire escape on the 2nd floor of the downtown building.
7. I stand in the open doorway from scene 6.
8. I repeat step 7, but this time I purposefully look down and get comfortable with this height. I also think about taking a step forward onto the platform of the fire escape.
9. I take one step out onto the platform of the fire escape. A friend is with me to provide support.
10. I repeat step 9, but this time I am alone.
11. I stand on the platform of the fire escape. A friend of mine walks up the fire escape to the 3rd floor.
12. I walk several steps on the fire escape up to the 3rd floor. My friend is with me.
13. I walk all the way up to the 3rd floor on the fire escape. My friend is with me.
14. I repeat step 13, but this time I am alone.
15. I imagine myself on a ski lift heading up the slope.
16. I actually go to the ski slopes with my friend. We take the ski lift together on the beginner's slope.
17. I take the beginner's ski lift by myself.
18. My friend and I take the ski lift on a more difficult slope.

19. I take the more difficult ski lift by myself.

Comments: People who are severely phobic often think there is nothing they could do to approach the feared object or situation. The first few items in this hierarchy help to illustrate the novel ways you can begin to gradually approach the relevant dimensions of your fear.

SAMPLE HIERARCHY FOR FEAR
OF DENTAL OR MEDICAL PROCEDURES

1. I look at pictures of a dentist's (physician's) office and think about visiting one with a friend. I wouldn't be examined, but would only look at things.
2. I talk with a friend of mine about a dental (medical) checkup just to get information. I choose a friend who is totally comfortable about visiting dentists (physicians).
3. I imagine visiting the professional's office with my friend. The dentist (physician) says hello to me and then examines my friend. I stay in the waiting room.
4. I actually go to the professional's office with my friend and meet the dentist (physician). I stay in the waiting room while my friend is examined.
5. On a subsequent occasion, I visit the professional with a friend and actually watch while the dentist (physician) checks over my friend's teeth (gives an injection, etc.).
6. I arrange with the professional to visit the office on my own. The dentist (physician) lets me sit in the dentist's chair (view the examination room) and explains each piece of equipment.
7. I visit the dentist's (physician's) office with my friend. This time I am examined while my friend is in the room. All the

procedures are explained to me and the doctor proceeds one step at a time.

8. I come back to the dentist (physician) for a series of mouth (chest) X rays. This time I visit alone.

9. I return to have a cavity filled (receive a vaccination). I visit on my own.

Comments: Once again the importance of using a model is illustrated. It should be noted that not every dentist or physician will agree to these procedures—but some might. If no one will cooperate, you will have to rely on imagined scenes. For the above hierarchy to be helpful, it is important that your friend and the doctor *not* pressure you. Remind them that you will gradually do things at a rate that is comfortable for you.

SAMPLE HIERARCHY FOR FEAR
OF PUBLIC SPEAKING

1. I practice reading from a book out loud while no one else is home.

2. I practice giving a spontaneous talk out loud while no one else is home.

3. I tape-record myself talking out loud. I then listen to the presentation.

4. I practice reading out loud to my family.

5. I practice reading out loud while a close friend is listening.

6. I practice giving a spontaneous talk while my close friend is listening. My friend gives me feedback on my performance and I practice again.

7. I imagine giving a talk to a group of friends. Initially I am nervous, but I imagine myself relaxing away my tension and controlling my breathing. The talk goes fairly well.

8. I imagine myself giving a talk to a group of strangers. My feelings of nervousness are under control and the talk goes fairly well.

9. I actually go to a group meeting with my friend. At this meeting I have something to say. I rehearse what I want to say and then I go ahead and speak to the group. My friend gives me feedback on how I did.

10. I repeat step 9 and try to improve my performance based on my friend's comments.

Comments: It is often observed that public speaking anxiety is affected by: (1) physical tension and breathing and (2) what speakers say to themselves. During imagined scenes it is useful to *rehearse* in your mind relaxation exercises and positive self-statements. An example of a positive self-statement is "If I control my breathing and concentrate on what I say, I know I can do this." This statement is certainly more productive than worrying to yourself, "Oh, my God, what do I do now?"

Naturally, your hierarchy items should cover whatever dimensions of the situation are important for you. Thus, the scenes can gradually increase the number of people present. Alternatively, your scenes could focus on the extent to which the people are strangers. Still other factors may be most relevant to your fear.

SAMPLE HIERARCHY FOR FEAR
OF JOB INTERVIEWS

1. A friend of mine who has been to job interviews tells me what is involved. I ask many questions and get a clear picture of what to expect.

2. I imagine that I am being interviewed for a job I really want. My friend is the interviewer and we have a friendly discussion.

3. I imagine that I am being interviewed for a job I really want. A stranger interviews me but acts in a friendly manner.

4. I imagine that I am being interviewed for a job I really want. A stranger interviews me and is rather formal.

5. I practice being interviewed in real life by having my friend interview me for an important job I want. My friend acts in a relaxed manner.

6. I repeat scene 5 and practice a job interview with my friend. This time my friend conducts a very formal interview.

7. I read the want ads and find a number of jobs that I would like to look into. I also find a number of jobs that I am qualified for but don't really want.

8. I call and make an appointment to be interviewed for a job I don't really want.

9. I call and make an appointment to be interviewed for a job I do want.

10. I go for an interview for the job I do not want.

11. I go for an interview for the job I would like to get.

Comments: The items in this hierarchy illustrate how you can practice a situation before trying it in the real world—by rehearsing it in your mind or by "playing it out" with a friend or relative. In this way you learn what to expect in real life. You also have an opportunity to get better at the things you need to do in the real situation. For example, when you imagine a job interview or practice an interview with your friend, you gain experience answering questions about yourself. With practice you improve your skills, and this will help you during an actual interview.

SAMPLE HIERARCHY FOR FEAR
OF SOCIAL DATING

1. I listen to my friend call someone for a date.

2. I have my friend describe what has been planned for the arranged date.
3. I imagine that I am with a group of people at a party. Someone comes up and talks to us. I ask a question and (s)he answers. I respond with a general positive comment like "I have felt the same way" or "That's a good point."
4. I imagine that I am with a group of people at a party. I get into an extended conversation with someone.
5. I imagine that at a party I get into an extended conversation with someone. At the end of our talk I ask the person out for a date.
6. I imagine that I am at home and I phone someone for a date. The person says (s)he is busy that evening, but (s)he would love to make it some other time.
7. I imagine that I am at home phoning someone for a date. The person says (s)he is busy, and (s)he does not suggest getting together another time.
8. I imagine that I phone someone for a date. The person says (s)he would love to go out. We then talk for several minutes to arrange a time and place.
9. I imagine myself spending an evening with the person I asked out. I picture myself driving to the house, greeting my date, and driving to the show (restaurant, club, etc.).
10. I go to a party with a group of friends. At the party I try to engage in a number of short conversations. As I practice this, I am not thinking about dates or more difficult situations. I am only trying to get comfortable with short "chitchat" conversations.
11. I am at a party and during a short conversation I find myself particularly interested in one individual. I maintain my conversation with this person for several minutes. I am still not thinking about a date. I only want to work on improving my conversational skills.
12. I imagine myself spending an evening with the person I liked at the party. I picture myself calling up and arranging the

date. I then imagine driving to the person's house, greeting my date, and driving to a show (restaurant, club, etc.).

13. I call the person I met at the party and ask if (s)he would like to meet for coffee some afternoon. I suggest a local restaurant that has a relaxed atmosphere.

14. I meet my date at the restaurant and we spend an hour together.

Comments: In several ways, fear of social dating is one of the more difficult fears to work with. First, there is always the possibility of rejection and the resulting feelings of failure. Second, and most importantly, successful social dating requires a number of skills. Thus, you not only need to feel relaxed while you are dating, you also need to now what to do. This is far different from the person afraid of flying in airplanes; in this case, the only required skill is sitting in a chair!

People who have a fear of social dating may not have as many social and conversational skills as they would like. This may be due to a lack of either past experiences or recent practice. Either way, people can supplement their strategy for approach with outside informational materials that illustrate what people do on dates. In this regard, you may want to start watching and listening to other people as they interact. "How-to" books that describe effective methods for dealing with difficult social situations can also be useful. You can probably find books on social dating at your local bookstore. Finally, television and movies can provide "models" for how people act with each other. However, with these last two informational sources, be sure to distinguish between constructive models and the more unusual characters Hollywood has created for our entertainment.

Once you know what to do (and how to do it), you can rehearse social situations in your imagination. This is the first step toward eliminating your feelings of anxiety. After you are comfortable when imagining a situation, you can begin to practice it in real life. Thus, the sequence of procedures you should follow involves: (1) identifying useful social skills; (2) rehearsing these skills by practicing imagined scenes; and (3) actually practicing social situations in real life. Naturally, the situations you learn about, imagine, and practice will be ordered in a hierarchical fashion. This allows you to begin with easy situations and gradually work up to more difficult and intimate settings.

SAMPLE HIERARCHY FOR FEAR
OF SPIDERS

1. I look at a color picture of a spider. The spider is small and at a distance.

2. I look at a color picture of a spider. The spider is a large one and the picture is a close-up.

3. My friend captures a small spider and has it in a jar. I look at the spider from a distance of 15 feet.

4. My friend captures a small spider and has it in a jar. I approach the jar all the way up to 5 feet.

5. My friend captures a small spider and has it in a jar. I approach to a distance of 5 feet. My friend lifts the jar lid and lets the spider crawl on the table for a few seconds. The spider is then placed back in the jar and the lid replaced.

6. My friend lets the same small spider out of the jar and it crawls on the table. I am 5 feet away and I take a couple of steps forward.

7-

10. My friend locates a larger spider and brings it over in a jar. I repeat steps 3 through 6 with this larger specimen.

11. I spot a spider in my house on the wall. Instead of leaving the room I stay where I am and carefully look at it.

12. I spot a spider in my house. I walk up to it so that I am only 5 feet away.

13. I walk up to a spider in my house so that I am only 3 feet away.

Comments: This hierachy does not solve the problem about what to do with spiders once you see them. Some people would want to kill spiders with perhaps a rolled-up newspaper. Others would prefer to remove the spider from the house without killing it. This can be accomplished by placing a jar over the spider and then sliding a card underneath to serve as a top. Either of these procedures (newspaper or "mercy jar") could be modeled by your friend during the various steps. You could then practice these steps yourself, first with small spiders and then with larger ones. Of course, some of you may prefer to let spiders live and stay in your house. In that case, you will be satisfied with the goal of getting comfortable when spiders are around.

SAMPLE HIERARCHY FOR FEAR
OF SNAKES

1. I write the word SNAKE in big letters on a piece of paper.

2. A book about snakes lies unopened on a table next to my chair.

3. A book about snakes is opened and resting on my lap. It is opened to a page that does not have any pictures on it.

4. I have opened the book to a page containing a small black-and-white photo of a medium-sized pet snake. I look at the picture for a few seconds and close the book.

5. I have opened the book and now I look at the picture for a full 10 seconds.

6. I turn to a large color photo of a snake in the same book.

7. I imagine seeing a live snake during a nature film on Tv. The pictures of the snake are small and black and white.

8. I imagine seeing a snake in a movie. The movie is in color, and there is a sequence showing the snake moving from a rock to a log.

9. I imagine that I see a snake in real life, but it is 20 feet away from me and it looks dead.

10. I imagine seeing a dead snake. I walk up to it and poke it with a stick.

11. I imagine seeing a live snake about 20 feet away. I stand still and it crawls away.

12. I go to the reptile house at the local zoo. I am with my family and I stand outside the entrance door.

13. I go inside the reptile house and stand 20 feet from a caged snake. I look at the snake for only a second.

14. I repeat step 13, but now I look at the snake for a full 10 seconds.

15. I go inside the reptile house and walk up to the caged snake. I look at the snake for just a second.

16. I repeat step 15, but this time I look at the snake for a full 10 seconds.

17. I am back at home and imagine that I am gardening and see a snake near me. It rustles in the leaves and crawls away.

18. I actually approach my garden and see a snake about 20 feet away.

19. I am in my garden and see a snake about 10 feet away from me. I quietly take three steps toward it.

20. I am gardening and see a snake nearby. It moves away as if very frightened and I remain in the garden.

Comments: The last few scenes in this hierarchy may be difficult to control in real life. Therefore, this individual may want to practice imagining each scene before actually approaching the garden. It might also be necessary to make several visits to the garden before a snake is actually seen.

After you have carefully reviewed the sample hierarchies, you are ready to start planning your own approach strategy. Initially it may be difficult to decide if a particular scene should be imagined or actually practiced. It may also be difficult to know whether or not to include friends and relatives. Don't worry about these decisions now. Simply make a judgment about what is *probably* going to be best. Your decisions aren't final until you complete all the procedural steps listed below.

PROCEDURAL OUTLINE FOR
HIERARCHY CONSTRUCTION

1. Decide on an initial scene that would cause only a little anxiety.
2. Decide on a final scene that represents something you would like to do if you weren't afraid.
3. Generate a tentative list of scenes between the first and last items in your hierarchy.
4. Check that the list of scenes relates to the relevant dimensions of the object or situation that upsets you.
5. Rate your scenes in terms of how anxious they make you.
6. Begin to finalize your hierarchy by choosing your final scenes.
7. Add descriptive details to each of your scenes.
8. Develop a list of "coping self-statements" that can be used with your scenes.

Today you will complete steps 1 and 2 of the Procedural Outline and begin working on step 3. Then, in your next session, you will complete the remaining steps for constructing an anxiety hierarchy.

STEP 1: INITIAL SCENE

To start your hierarchy, think of a scene that would potentially cause you only a slight degree of tension. Be sure the scene is not very upsetting, since you want to be able to relax away any anxiety it may produce. Thus, if you are afraid of swimming, your hierarchy could start with a scene in which you are standing twenty feet from the edge of a pool. If that makes you too anxious, you could have a scene in which you simply *imagine* you are in this situation. Of course, it is possible that standing twenty feet from the edge of a pool wouldn't bother you at all. In that case you would pick a more difficult situation, such as walking up to the pool's edge.

The sample hierarchies should further clarify what your first scene can be like. The important rule to remember is this:

*Whatever your fear may be, your first scene should
evoke very little anxiety. If you make an error
in judgment, make this error on the side of too
little anxiety.*

Go ahead and decide on your first scene. Then write it down on p. 85, which is a Worksheet for formulating an initial list of hierarchy items.

STEP 2: FINAL SCENE

The last scene in your hierarchy should involve a situation that would probably create large amounts of anxiety if you actually practiced it now. Don't worry about whether you can relax to this last scene; and don't be concerned if it seems like you never could. Remember that you won't actually work on the latter scenes in your hierarchy until the very end of your program. When that time arrives, these scenes will be less frightening than they are now.

The sample hierarchies illustrate how your last scene should involve *close* contact with the object or situation that you fear. The general rule for deciding on your final scene is this:

> *Whatever your fear may be, your final scene should involve something you would really want to do if your fear was totally eliminated. If you make an error in judgment, make this error on the side of too much anxiety.*

Some of you may be so anxious that you refuse even to think of a final scene involving close contact with your feared object or situation. Usually this is not the case; most people can bring themselves to at least *talk* about their fear. (Remember that you aren't actually practicing anything yet.) However, if you are so fearful that thinking of a final scene is too upsetting, then you should think of the most anxiety-evoking scene you are *willing* to call to mind. Let this scene serve as the final one in your hierarchy. It will be your *first goal.* After you have learned to feel totally comfortable with all the situations leading up to your first goal, you will be able to start a new hierarchy. This second hierarchy will take you to your second or *final goal.* Although the scenes in your second hierarchy are difficult to think about now, they will be significantly less troublesome when you have successfully completed your first goal.

Once you have decided on your final scene, write it down on the Worksheet. Then return to the instructions below.

STEPS 3 AND 4:
ADDITIONAL SCENES RELEVANT TO YOUR FEAR

Your first and last scenes have defined the "end points" of your anxiety hierarchy. Now you want to generate a list of scenes

**WORK SHEET FOR STARTING
YOUR ANXIETY HIERARCHY**

First Scene: THIS SCENE SHOULD EVOKE ONLY THE VERY SMALLEST AMOUNTS OF ANXIETY.

Last Scene: THIS SCENE WOULD PROBABLY MAKE YOU VERY ANXIOUS IF YOU ACTUALLY PRACTICED IT. THE SCENE SHOULD INVOLVE CLOSE CONTACT WITH THE FEARED OBJECT OR SITUATION.

List of Additional Scenes:

_____

_____

_____

_____

_____

_____

_____

_____

_____

_____

_____

Use additional paper if your hierarchy contains more items.

to cover the full range of your anxiety reactions. Using the Worksheet and additional paper, write down as many as twenty-five or thirty tentative scenes. These scenes should fall between the end points of your hierarchy so they gradually take you from the first to the last item. This is what is meant by "covering the full range of your anxiety reactions."

The following examples are to remind you that your scenes need to relate to the relevant dimensions of your fear. Consider a man who is afraid of social gatherings because he is upset by crowds. This man's hierarchy scenes should involve a gradual increase in the number of people present. However, another individual may be anxious at social gatherings because he is afraid of females. In this instance, an anxiety hierarchy based on the number of people present would be less relevant. This second individual would want to develop a list of scenes that increased his imagined and practiced contact with females in a variety of settings. Finally, a third person may be afraid of social gatherings because he has a drinking problem and becomes anxious when alcoholic beverages are available. Neither of the previous hierarchies would be relevant for him.

We could probably list a dozen reasons why people feel anxious at social gatherings. The point is that people have to know the relevant dimensions of their fears if they want to construct successful strategies for approach. Remember this as you generate your initial list of hierarchy items. Use the Assessment Sheet you previously completed as a reminder of the important dimensions of your fear.

Between now and your next regular session, spend some time each day adding to your list of scenes. Some of you may want to get help from friends or members of your family. These people can make it more fun as you creatively combine imagined, real-life, and modeled situations into an approach strategy.

STOP!

Do not continue to the next set of instructions until you have generated an initial list of hierarchy scenes. Have this list completed before your next regular session.

STEP 5: RATING YOUR SCENES

This is your second session on hierarchy construction, and today you will probably complete your approach strategy. The next step in the procedure is to rate how anxious each of your initial scenes would probably make you feel if they were actually practiced now. To help you do this, think of a scale in which the whole numbers between 0 and 100 (0, 1, 2, etc. up through 98, 99, 100) represent *subjective units of discomfort.* Now let's say the bottom of your scale is 0, representing the lowest level of anxiety you could ever feel. In fact, let 0 equal "no anxiety" or "completely relaxed." Then make the top of your scale stand for extreme anxiety, so that 100 equals "as much anxiety as you have ever experienced."

You now want to think about how much discomfort each scene on your list would cause you to feel. Start off by rating the first and last scenes, since these mark the end points of your hierarchy. After you make your ratings, it may be necessary to modify the scenes themselves. For example, if your subjective rating of the initial scene is more than 5 you should probably think of a different scene that evokes less anxiety. This is because your first scene should create only the very smallest amount of tension. Any error in your judgment here should be in the direction of *too little* anxiety.

As regards your last scene, it is likely that your rating will be quite high. That doesn't mean you need to rate it at 100; your anxiety about a feared object or situation may simply not be that great. But it is likely that the last scene in your hierarchy will evoke a good deal of tension, and your discomfort rating should reflect this.

After the first and last scenes have been rated, go on to the remaining items on your initial list. Then, order the rated scenes according to how uncomfortable they make you. If, for example, four of your scenes are rated 36, 42, 61, and 55, you should rearrange the last two scenes. Have them listed so they continue to gradually increase in an orderly manner. Once you have arranged your scenes in this way, you are ready to finalize your hierarchy.

STEP 6:
CHOOSING YOUR FINAL SCENES

To finalize your hierarchy you first want to eliminate un-necessary or redundant scenes. In general, *adjacent scenes should differ in their ratings by at least 3, but should never be more than 7 apart.* This guideline probably allows you to drop several scenes from your initial list that are very similar to adjacent items.

It is also likely that some scenes are too *dissimilar* from adjacent items so that new scenes will need to be created. This can often be accomplished by simply combining details from scenes already on your list. For example, let's assume that a man afraid of bees has chosen the following two adjacent scenes:

1. I am resting outside and I hear a distant buzzing sound. (Rating = 60)
2. I see a bee hovering five feet away from me. (Rating = 70)

(Naturally, some people afraid of bees would select different ratings or might even want to reverse the order of these items. The ratings given here are only examples.)

As they now stand, the sample adjacent scenes are too far apart. Because their ratings differ by more than 7 points, the man is likely to experience a sizable increase in anxiety when he proceeds from the first to the second situation. Accordingly, he should create a new scene that falls between these two. To do this he can combine elements from each of the scenes and imagine the following: I hear a buzzing sound and see a bee flying *away* from me (Rating = 66). This new scene increases the man's anxiety associated with simply hearing a buzz (scene 1). At the same time, the scene decreases his anxiety associated with a hovering bee whose direction of flight is unknown (scene 2).

There are several ways to decrease the anxiety caused by a particular situation. You can:

1. imagine the scene rather than actually practice it;
2. include a friend or relative;
3. increase the distance between you and the situation;
4. shorten the time interval during which you expose yourself to the situation; or
5. approach smaller or less threatening versions of the thing you fear.

You should consider these strategies whenever it is necessary to decrease or increase your ratings. After you have eliminated redundant scenes and checked that all adjacent items have ratings 3 to 7 units apart, you can go on to the next step in your program.

STEP 7: ADDING DETAILS

Your next job is to add details to the final scenes so you know exactly how to practice them. To appreciate how important this step is, let's begin with a discussion of imagined scenes. Even if you aren't using them in your hierarchy, the following points are important.

When you practice a scene in real life, you obviously are an active participant. As it turns out, it is just as important to actively participate in imagined situations. Unfortunately, most people who imagine scenes make the mistake of passively observing themselves "from the outside." For example, a man afraid of airplanes might imagine *seeing himself* standing ten feet from a jet. Contrast this approach to one in which the man imagines *what it would feel like* if he actually were ten feet from the plane. Instead of passively observing himself in the scene, he would experience himself standing on the concrete, looking at the jet, hearing the noises of the airport around him, and feeling a sense of activity all around. Suddenly he is involved and actively participating in the situation.

During your treatment sessions you want to adopt an active approach to visualizing scenes. Try to put yourself in the scene as if you are really there. To do this, you need to add sufficient details to each of your situations. The following scene demonstrates why this is so important:

Imagine that you're sitting on a beach by the ocean.
Try to make the scene alive so it really feels like
you're there.

Close your eyes and experience this scene as vividly as you can. Hold the image for about ten seconds and then return to the instructions below.

Hopefully you experienced the previous scene as if you were really on the beach. But did you add sufficient details to stimulate your senses? Did you imagine how it feels when the ocean breeze touches you? Did you imagine the sound of the waves? the smell of the ocean? the texture of the sand? Did you include the expansive feeling of viewing the horizon all around you, and the contrast of white, billowy clouds against a clear blue sky? Did you feel the hot sun beating down on your back—or was it on your side?

Visualize the beach scene again, and this time add as many details as you can. Really experience the scene as an active participant.

Do you see the difference this can make?

To further illustrate this point, you will find revised sample hierarchies for fear of dental procedures and fear of public speaking on pp. 93-96. Each of the scenes in these hierarchies has added details not included in the original hierarchies on pp. 73 and 74.

Once you have studied the sample hierarchies you are ready to return to your own list of scenes. Spend some time adding details that will make each scene seem as real as possible. Doing this for imagined situations makes it easier to vividly experience them. Just as important, adding details to real-life situations helps you know how to better practice them. By the way, adding details can affect your original discomfort ratings; so remember to check them. If a scene has been significantly changed, either modify your ratings or redefine the situation.

When you have added sufficient details, copy each of your scenes down on pp. 97-98. This will provide you with a list of final hierarchy items.

REVISED HIERARCHY FOR FEAR
OF DENTAL PROCEDURES

1. I get a dentistry magazine from my local library and look through the articles. When a picture of a dentist's office comes up, I look at it and try to get comfortable thinking about seeing one in person. I focus on the colors, the equipment, and the people.

2. I talk to a friend of mine (Bill) about my fear of dentists and ask him to describe what a visit is like. I have chosen to speak to Bill because he is *not* afraid of dentists and he is very good at explaining things *clearly*. Bill describes for me everything, including the sounds of the office, the feeling of sitting in the dentist's chair, and other details that affect my perceptions.

3. I sit in the comfortable chair I have used for my relaxation training. I close my eyes and imagine that I am visiting the dentist's office with Bill. I stay in the waiting room while Bill is seen for a checkup. I am there about 20 minutes. I see the magazine in my lap; there are other people waiting; and the receptionist is answering the phone and greeting people as they arrive. At the end of Bill's checkup, the dentist greets me and says hello. He looks just the way Bill described.

4. I actually practice step 3 in real life when Bill goes for his checkup.

5. I arrange with another friend of mine to go to the dentist and I watch while my friend's teeth are examined. I see the dentist checking over my friend's mouth and taking a set of dental X rays. My friend seems calm, although it looks like it would be tiring to keep my mouth opened that long. The office is well lit and very clean. The dentist seems efficient and does his job with confidence.

6. I call up the dentist and arrange to visit his office on my own. The dentist greets me in the waiting room and then we go to his examination room. I sit in the chair and relax away any tension I might be feeling. I remind myself that nothing is happening—I am only getting comfortable with the situation and learning what the chair feels like. The dentist explains to me the various pieces of equipment: drills, grinders, water faucets, X ray equipment, and other devices.

7. I return to the dentist's office with Bill. This time I am examined while Bill stands nearby. The doctor is very helpful and proceeds one step at a time. He explains everything he is doing. We have arranged for a 40-minute examination so he will not be rushed.

8. I return to the dentist and have a series of mouth X rays. Because I am now familiar with the procedures and the office, I visit alone.

9. I visit the dentist on my own and have a medium-sized cavity filled. The cavity was revealed by my X rays. The procedure takes about 30 minutes.

REVISED HIERARCHY FOR FEAR
OF PUBLIC SPEAKING

1. I am alone at home. Standing up in my living room I read out loud from my reference book on elections in the 1960s. I read two pages and try to modulate my voice and keep my posture straight.

2. I use the same reference book as my source of information. This time I stand in my living room and try to give a spontaneous talk on elections in the 1960s. No one else is at home, but I imagine people in front of me. I try to really feel what it would be like if I were on stage.

3. I repeat step 2, but this time I tape-record my speech. I then listen to the presentation, think of some ways to improve my performance, and repeat the talk.

4. I read out loud from the election book as in step 1, but this time my husband is present. He is sitting in a chair about five feet in front of me.

5. I again read out loud from the election book as in step 1, but this time my friend Doris is with me. I am comfortable with Doris, but not as relaxed as I was with my husband. Doris is sitting in the same chair as my husband used in step 4. I make an effort to get relaxed by breathing evenly and taking short pauses at the end of each paragraph. I also systematically practice my positive coping self-statments.

6. I practice again with Doris but now I give a spontaneous talk instead of reading from the book. I speak for five minutes about a recent experience I had with mutual friends. Doris gives me feedback on my performance and I practice again. This time I talk about a more formal topic.

7. I am sitting in the comfortable chair that I used for relaxation training. I close my eyes and get relaxed. I then imagine that I am giving a talk to a group of friends. I am speaking about the elections in the 1960s and I see my friends listening to me. They seem interested. I imagine myself taking even breaths, watching my posture, and speaking in a moderately even and relaxed tone. I also imagine that I am initially nervous but my tension declines as the talk continues. The room is well lit but warm. There is cigarette smoke in the air. I notice people shuffling in their chairs. Sometimes I hear someone cough.

8. I repeat step 7 but this time imagine that I am giving my talk to students in the political science class I am taking. I see

the students in front of me. The teacher is sitting in the back of the room. The clock is on the wall to my right. The room is well lit, the air is warm and smoky. At times I hear people shuffling in their chairs or coughing. I try to maintain eye contact with some of the people.

9. I actually go to my course with Doris. At this meeting I have a question in mind. I rehearse exactly what I want to say and then I raise my hand. The teacher recognizes me and I ask the question. I then concentrate on listening to the teacher's answer. After class my friend gives me feedback on how I did.

10. I repeat step 9 and try to improve my performance based on my friend's comments.

STEP 8: SELF-STATEMENTS

The list of scenes you have just completed makes it possible to approach the thing you fear in a gradual manner. At the same time, your relaxation skills can counter body tension that might otherwise occur when you practice your scenes. In this way, your anxiety hierarchy and relaxation program can be effective in changing overt behaviors and physical responses.

But remember that a third component to fearful behavior exists and must be changed—your *self-statements*. What people say to themselves can play an important role in maintaining their fears. For example, when "test-anxious" people come across difficult questions during an examination, they often "freeze" on the spot. Their thoughts become blocked and they don't know what to do. Studies have shown that many of these people are saying to themselves negative statements such as "I'm stupid," "I have no idea what the answer is," "I can never do this right," or "I'm so nervous, what can I do?"

When test-anxious individuals learn to talk to themselves in more helpful ways, they often feel less anxious. Their grades can

LIST OF
FINAL HIERARCHY SCENES

SCENE	DESCRIPTION	DISCOMFORT RATING
1		
2		
3		
4		
5		
6		
7		
8		
9		
10		
11		
12		

SCENE	DESCRIPTION	SUDS RATING
13		
14		
15		
16		

Use additional paper if your hierarchy contains more items.

even improve significantly. Rather than worrying about a difficult question, they learn to say: "This looks like a tricky problem. Now, let's see how to approach it. First I'll get relaxed and then I'll think about what the question really asks. OK. This question seems most related to the materials I read about in the text. I should be able to solve it if I first . . ."

See the difference between self-statements which maintain anxiety and ones which help you cope with a situation? Perhaps you can think of examples related to your fear. Those of you afraid of an animal or insect may say to yourselves, "Oh, my God, it's going to attack me—I want to scream." Now what if instead you were to say: "Hmmm, that is a curious-looking thing. It certainly startled me at first, but it doesn't seem to be doing much of anything"—?

If you are afraid of driving, boating, or some other form of travel, you may say to yourself, "What if there is an accident? I can't handle this situation." Would it not be more constructive if you could instead say; "The driver (navigator) seems to have perfect control over this vehicle. I don't think there is any realistic reason to worry, so I'll try to get relaxed"—?

Those of you afraid of social situations who say, "They don't like me" or "I'm looking bad" should consider statements like "I know what I want to say. If I just get relaxed, I can start enjoying myself."

As part of your treatment program, take a few minutes to develop a list of constructive and positive self-statements. These statements serve two functions. First, they help you feel more relaxed in difficult situations. In this respect, a statement like "I can relax if I want to" is a lengthier version of the cue words used during relaxation training. Remember, what you say to yourself plays an important part in how you feel and what you do.

The second function that positive self-statements serve is to help you *cope* with problems or difficult situations. Positive statements help you do this by directing your attention to the realistic demands of a situation. In this way you attend to the goal you want to achieve and *not* to your worries. This is precisely what the test-anxious individuals were learning to do in our previous example.

On p. 101 space is provided for you to generate a list of self-statements that can help eliminate your fear or phobia. First, list all the negative and worrisome statements you now make on the left-hand side of the page. After listing these *nonproductive* statements, use the right-hand side of the page to record a list of constructive expressions. Remember that your constructive statements can help you relax and cope with situations in your anxiety hierarchy. In this respect, saying to yourself, "Isn't everything wonderful?" will prove less helpful than saying, "If I get relaxed and think about my behavior, I know I can do better."

After completing your lists of negative and positive statements, you are ready to begin the last step of your treatment program. All the preliminary work has been finished: you can counter tension with relaxation; you can stop avoiding things by employing a strategy of gradual approach; and you can replace your worries with coping self-statements.

SELF-STATEMENTS LIST

NEGATIVE—WORRYING

On this side of the page you should write down the type of statements you typically make to yourself when you are anxious and confronted by the object or situation that you fear.

POSITIVE—COPING

On this side of the page you should write down the type of statements you *could* make to yourself *if* you were constructively coping with the object or situation that you fear.

Examples:

I'm so terrified . . .
What can I do . . .
I've got to get away . . .
I'm so embarrassed . . .
I'll never get over this . . .

Examples:

I want to calm down . . .
I can relax if I try . . .
I can cope with this . . .
Let me focus on what I can do here . . .
I'm feeling better . . .

Your Statements:

1. _____

_____

_____

2. _____

_____

_____

3. _____

_____

_____

4. _____

_____

_____

5. _____

_____

_____

Your Statements:

1. _____

_____

_____

2. _____

_____

_____

3. _____

_____

_____

4. _____

_____

_____

5. _____

_____

_____

Use additional paper if more space is needed.

6

OVERCOMING YOUR FEAR OR PHOBIA

This chapter provides a set of rules for combining your relaxation skills, coping statements, and anxiety hierarchy. Underlying these rules is the general principle of fear reduction presented in Chapter 2:

Feeling comfortable while exposure is maintained can help you overcome your fear or phobia.

Because you last considered this principle several weeks ago, let's review how it applies to your program. Remember that people act in ways that maintain their fears and phobias; when faced by an upsetting object or situation, they try to escape. In this way people teach themselves that exposure is distressful and only escape brings relief. Your program breaks up this sequence and teaches you to remain comfortable *while* exposure is maintained. You do this by using your relaxation skills and coping self-statements while gradually approaching the object or situation you fear.

The rules outlined in this chapter teach you how to combine the various parts of your program into a successful treatment package. Spend today's session studying these rules carefully. Then, in your *next* regularly scheduled session you will begin the process of overcoming your fear or phobia.

SCHEDULING SESSIONS

To help you schedule your sessions and track your progress, a new set of Log Sheets is provided at the end of this chapter (pp. 113-114). Your sessions will be greatly influenced by the type of scenes you practice and the ways you react to them. Whatever the situation, a number of general guidelines apply:

1. Continue to hold at least two regularly scheduled sessions each week.

2. Avoid having your sessions run any longer than forty minutes.

3. Never complete more than five hierarchy scenes in a single session. This ensures that your rate of progress will be reasonably paced and gradual.

4. Begin your *first* session with the least fearful scene in your hierarchy (scene 1). In subsequent sessions, begin with the last scene successfully completed in the preceding session. For example, if you complete scenes 8 through 11 during session 4, session 5 will begin with scene 11.

5. Always end your sessions with a successfully completed scene. If you are working on scene 6 at the end of a session and you feel somewhat anxious, go back and prac-

tice scene 5. That way you will end your session with a successful experience and a greater sense of relaxation.

HOW TO PRACTICE HIERARCHY ITEMS

BE ACTIVE

Whether you practice real-life situations or imagined scenes, it is important to be involved in them. Visualize imagined scenes as vividly as you can; let your senses respond to the details that are supposed to be around you; and try to feel as if you are actually participating in the situation.

BE RELAXED

Before starting any scene, you want to get comfortable and relaxed. It also helps to take a short "relaxation break" after a scene is practiced. Relaxation breaks after imagined scenes can be about twenty seconds, after real-life situations about one or two minutes.

PRACTICE A SCENE IF YOU ARE NOT ANXIOUS

If you remain relaxed while vividly experiencing an imagined scene, then hold the image for a full fifteen seconds. Naturally, the times spent with real-life situations are more variable: you may drive around the neighborhood for five minutes, or you may sit in a car for only thirty seconds. The important point with real-life situations is that their length is *always* to be determined *in advance*. Have *every* detail worked out so you know when to start, what to do, and when to stop.

Every scene in your hierarchy should be practiced at least twice. If on two consecutive trials you do *not* feel anxious, you can proceed to the next scene on your list. Thus, if your hierarchy consists of sixteen items and you never experience anxiety during any of your sessions, you will finish the program in only thirty-two trials. Of course, that has probably never happened in the entire clinical history of this treatment! Almost everyone experiences some anxiety at some point in their program.

TRY TO COPE WITH SLIGHT TENSION

The scenes in your hierarchy will sometimes cause you to feel slight tension that quickly passes on its own. On other occasions, tension may persist unless you actively relax it away. When this happens, remember to use your relaxation skills and coping self-statements. For example, imagine you are approaching a feared object and you begin to feel uncomfortable. You may be able to cope with the situation by thinking to yourself: "My body is getting tense. If I exhale evenly and think about what I am doing, I can probably master this situation. Just relax and think about my next step. Nothing terrible is happening. I can actually do pretty well when I try."

Such coping skills will often overcome feelings of slight tension. When they are effective, you can practice your scenes for the full trial periods originally planned. Note, however, that practice trials during which you feel tense *do not* count as one of the two consecutive trials required for progressing to the next scene.

IMMEDIATELY STOP WHEN
UNCOMFORTABLY TENSE

There are likely to be times when you feel uncomfortably tense during an imagined scene or real-life situation. *Uncomfortably tense* refers to tension or anxiety that is noticeable, does not pass quickly, and cannot be successfully relaxed away. The occurence of uncomfortable tension does not mean you are failing at your program. All it means is that your strategy for approach is proceeding too rapidly; the distances between adjacent hierarchy items are greater than you anticipated.

When a scene makes you feel uncomfortably tense, you should *immediately stop* your practice trial and go back to relaxing. At times, people find it difficult to get a troubling scene out of their minds. If this happens, try thinking of a pleasant scene such as lying on the beach on a warm summer day. Focus on this alternative scene *and* use your relaxation skills to regain a sense of comfort. However long it takes, spend the necessary time getting relaxed. Never go on to a new scene while you still feel anxious.

Once you are feeling relaxed again, give the difficult scene a second try. It is always possible that repeated practice will decrease your feelings of anxiety and then you will be on your way to mastering the scene. It may take three trials, five trials, or more. But as long as anxiety diminishes from one trial to the next, you will eventually get relaxed in the situation.

When a scene makes you tense and your anxiety does *not* decrease with continued practice, there is no point in continuing with that scene. *Do not repeatedly practice scenes that cause non-diminishing anxiety reactions.* Instead construct a new item for your hierarchy. This item (and its discomfort rating) should fall between your last successfully completed scene and the one that repeatedly makes you anxious. Thus, if you were made anxious by scene 6 in your hierarchy, you would construct a new scene numbered 5½. Constructing this scene will create a more manageable "jump" or "gap" between scenes 5 and 6.

Scenes that are added to your program are practiced in the same way as your original hierarchy items. If you practiced scene 5½ and remained relaxed on two consecutive trials, you would move on to scene 6. If you felt uncomfortably tense while practicing scene 5½, you would have to construct still another scene for your hierarchy—scene 5¼.

If constructing new items causes you trouble, refer back to

Chapter 5. On p. 91 there are a number of guidelines to help you decrease the anxiety caused by a particular scene.

REVIEWING THE RULES

To help you learn the rules just outlined, there is a Summary Rule Sheet on p. 108-109. Following this is a Decision Flowchart (p. 111) that diagrams how to practice each of your hierarchy items. Study these items carefully.

When you feel you have adequately learned the materials, take the quiz on p. 109. If *any* questions on this quiz are missed, you should *definitely* spend more time studying the instructions in this chapter. The correct answers to the questions appear at the bottom of p. 115.

SUMMARY OF RULES

SCHEDULING SESSIONS

1. Hold two sessions weekly. Sessions should never be longer than forty minutes.
2. Never complete more than five scenes in a single session.
3. Begin session 1 with your first scene. Begin subsequent sessions with the last successfully completed scene from the preceding session.
4. Always end sessions with a successfully completed item.

HOW TO PRACTICE HIERARCHY ITEMS

1. Be an active participant in both imagined and real-life situations.

2. Be relaxed before starting a scene.

3. When you practice a scene and remain relaxed, continue the scene for the planned period (imagined scenes for fifteen seconds; real-life situations are variable).

4. When you practice a scene and feel tension, try to relax it away. If you are uncomfortably tense, immediately stop your practice trial.

5. When you successfully practice a scene and remain relaxed on two consecutive trials, move on to the next hierarchy item.

6. When you practice a scene and feel tense, repeat this scene as long as your anxiety reactions diminish. If you experience nondiminishing anxiety, then construct a new scene for your hierarchy. Practice this new scene as you would any other.

QUIZ

Consider the following situations and decide what you should do.

1. You are working on scene 6 of your hierarchy and you begin to feel slightly anxious. You should:
   (*a*) immediately stop the scene
   (*b*) continue to practice and experience the anxiety as much as possible
   (*c*) continue to practice only if you can relax away your tension
   (*d*) continue to practice but for half the regular time period.

2. You are working on scene 6 and are fully relaxed. The second time you practice this scene you also remain comfortable. you should:
   (*a*) practice scene 6 again
   (*b*) move on to scene 7
   (*c*) move back to scene 5
   (*d*) construct a new scene between scenes 5 and 6.

3. You are working on scene 6 for the first time and suddenly feel uncomfortably tense. You should:
   (*a*) immediately stop the scene
   (*b*) continue to practice and experience the anxiety as much as possible
   (*c*) immediately practice the next scene from your hierarchy.
   (*d*) continue to practice, but for half the regular time period.

4. You have practiced scene 6 twice, and on both occasions you have felt an equally large degree of tension. You should:
   (*a*) practice scene 6 again
   (*b*) move on to scene 7
   (*c*) move back to scene 5
   (*d*) construct a new scene between scenes 5 and 6.

5. You have practiced scene 6 twice, and on both occasions you have felt anxious. However, your anxiety was less the second time. You should:
   (*a*) practice scene 6 again
   (*b*) move on to scene 7
   (*c*) move back to scene 5
   (*d*) construct a new scene between scenes 5 and 6.

6. You have practiced scene 6 several times. Every time you have worked on this scene you have felt anxious, but each trial was associated with a reduction in your tension. Then, after four more trials, you experience an increase in your level of anxiety. You should:
   (*a*) practice scene 6 again
   (*b*) move on to scene 7
   (*c*) move back to scene 5
   (*d*) construct a new scene between scenes 5 and 6.

DECISION FLOW CHART

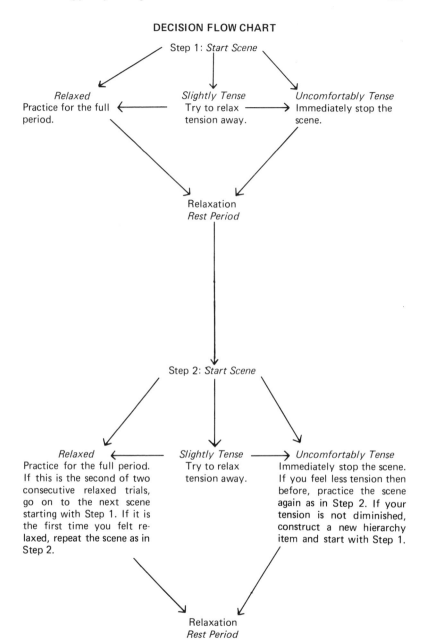

Step 1: *Start Scene*

Relaxed
Practice for the full period.

Slightly Tense
Try to relax tension away.

Uncomfortably Tense
Immediately stop the scene.

Relaxation
Rest Period

Step 2: *Start Scene*

Relaxed
Practice for the full period. If this is the second of two consecutive relaxed trials, go on to the next scene starting with Step 1. If it is the first time you felt relaxed, repeat the scene as in Step 2.

Slightly Tense
Try to relax tension away.

Uncomfortably Tense
Immediately stop the scene. If you feel less tension then before, practice the scene again as in Step 2. If your tension is not diminished, construct a new hierarchy item and start with Step 1.

Relaxation
Rest Period

GETTING STARTED

You can now begin to work at overcoming your fear or phobia. Spend as many sessions as it takes to complete all the items in your anxiety hierarchy. To keep track of your progress, use the Log Sheets on pp. 113 and 114.

By the way, if your program does not always proceed as smoothly as you expect, don't throw your hands in the air and say, "What's the use? I can't do this!" Stay calm and use your coping skills to analyze the situation. Try to relate any difficulties you are having to the basic steps of your program. For example, if you are unable to relax away small amounts of tension during a hierarchy scene, consider returning to Chapter 4. It might only take you a short session to brush up on relaxation skills.

If you are unable to progress through several hierarchy items, it may be that your discomfort ratings are off, that the gaps between adjacent scenes are too great. Alternatively, you may have failed to construct items that adequately cover the relevant dimensions of your fear. In either case, you would want to refer back to Chapter 5 and consider rebuilding portions of your hierarchy.

The point of the above examples is this: *If something does go wrong, think carefully about your program and what is happening.* Analyze the steps in your procedure and make a *constructive* change in one of them. By doing this and using your coping skills, you should be able to overcome difficulties as they occur. Although this may sound as though it is easier said then done, *you really can be a good problem solver when you try.* You can figure out what is wrong if you take the time to think about things patiently and carefully.

When you have completed practicing all the items in your hierarchy, return to this book and read the last chapter (Chapter 7). This last chapter will help you assess how much you have

LOG SHEET FOR OVERCOMING
YOUR FEAR OR PHOBIA

For *general instructions* see your Summary Rule Sheet and Decision Flow Chart.

DATE OF SESSION	WHAT WAS PRACTICED	LAST SCENE
Feb. 14	Started with scene 1 from my hierarchy. Did three scenes today.	3
Feb. 17	Started with scene 3. Got to scene 5, but had to make a new item after scene 4 (#4½).	5
Feb. 21	Started with scene 5. Moved rapidly through to scene 9.	9

DATE OF SESSION	WHAT WAS PRACTICED	LAST SCENE

changed. It will also assist you in planning additional steps that can be practiced in the future.

You are now on your own. Good luck—and work hard. If any questions arise during your practice, refer back to the relevant sections of this program.

Answer Key:
1. (*c*)   4. (*d*)
2. (*b*)   5. (*a*)
3. (*a*)   6. (*d*)

7

HOW MUCH HAVE
YOU CHANGED?

This chapter is for your use *after* you have completed the entire treatment program. If you have reached this point you are probably asking yourself, "Well, have I changed?" The present chapter helps you answer this question with more precision than simply yes or no. In that way you can better understand what has, and what has not, changed. You will also know where to go from here.

On p. 119 you will find a copy of the Assessment Sheet that you originally filled out when constructing your anxiety hierarchy. You should complete this new form now according to how you are currently feeling. It is very important that you do this *without looking back* at your original sheet. Later on the two forms will be compared to see how you have changed; but for now, don't let your past reactions influence any of your present ratings.

Start the Assessment Sheet by filling in a general heading for your fear (item 1). Then list those characteristics of the feared object or situation that still upset you (item 2). After that, take a couple of minutes to order the relevant characteristics of your fear according to their current importance.

In the next part of the Assessment Sheet (item 3) list recent experiences that involved the object or situation you fear. Many of you have probably had relevant experiences outside the context of your treatment program. If you have, then include these. If not, you will want to consider any recent practice you have had with hierarchy scenes.

As you think about your recent experiences, consider what you *said* to yourself, how you *acted*, and how you *felt*. Write these things down under the heading "Your Reactions" (item 4).

All that remains to complete your current assessment is a "General Fear Rating" (item 5). Ask yourself to what extent the object or situation you originally feared still bothers you. The rating scale is exactly the same as the one used at the beginning of your program. The higher your number (further to the right), the more you are afraid and distressed. The lower your number (further to the left), the less afraid you are.

Now that you have completed the Assessment Sheet, turn back to p. 61 and compare your current responses to your original ones. Note whether the same dimensions or characteristics of your fear are still upsetting you. Compare how you used to react to difficult situations with how you now react. Do you still say to yourself, "I can't do this, I'm so afraid"? Or are you saying things like, "I've really changed. I can control this situation"? Do you still run away from situations, or are you remaining calm and continuing your normal activities? With regard to how you used to feel, is your heart still throbbing and is your stomach still tightening up? Or are you now remaining relatively relaxed?

Take a minute to think about the *specific behaviors* that used to characterize your fear or phobia. You can now see why a simple yes-or-no answer to the question "Have I changed?" is really inadequate. Most fears are never totally "cured" or totally

ASSESSMENT SHEET

1. Feared object or situation: _____
2. Important Characteristics:

	Rank		Rank
1 _____	___	6 _____	___
2 _____	___	7 _____	___
3 _____	___	8 _____	___
4 _____	___	9 _____	___
5 _____	___	10 _____	___

3. Past Experiences:

4. Your Reactions:
   Self-report (saying):

   Overt behavior (acting):

   Physical (feeling):

5. General Fear Rating: Indicate how anxious you get when you have contact with the object or situation you fear.

0	1	2	3	4	5	6	7	8	9	10

Truly
Not Upset

Moderately
Upset

As Upset as I
Could Ever Be

changed. In fact, if I were to ask someone, "How much have you changed as a result of treatment?" I would expect them to tell me:

> Well, the program has greatly reduced my physical feelings of tension. My heart doesn't pound, and I don't perspire like I used to. I can do almost everything I want, although in difficult situations I still worry about things and feel a little uncomfortable.

Or:

> I now do many things I never could do before. But my stomach is still tight, and physically I feel on edge. This makes it difficult for me to feel really comfortable.

Or:

> Very little has changed. I guess I do a few more things and sometimes feel less tense. But I still worry to myself; and I certainly can't get relaxed when I keep going over in my mind how nervous I am.

In the first answer to my question "How much have you changed?" the person appears to be saying that things have gone very well. Continued experience and contact with the feared object or situation is likely to extend the treatment gains this person has already experienced. Within this framework, you can think of situations that remain difficult for you as *extensions* of your original hierarchy. If such a situation should arise, remember to apply the same procedures that have been used all along.

The second answer to my question presents a different situation. In this case, the person is able to approach many new things but still feels physically tense. This suggests that additional work in relaxation skills is needed before the person practices more difficult situations.

The third person responding to my question might have

been tempted to answer by simply saying, "No, I haven't changed." But actually, *some* situations had improved. It also appears that anxious self-statements are especially important in maintaining the uncomfortable feelings. It would probably help if this person practiced difficult hierarchy items while concentrating on the use of positive, coping self-statements.

Your response to treatment may have been totally different from any of these examples. To evaluate what has changed for *you*, answer the following questions regarding various aspects of your fear or phobia.

1. In what specific situations do you feel more comfortable?

2. In what situations are you still tense?

3. What behaviors have changed for you? In what ways are you doing, saying, or feeling different things?

4. Do the same characteristics of your feared object or situation still upset you? Or are you now anxious about other factors that weren't really covered during treatment?

Your answers to the previous questions can tell you how much you have changed and what you should consider doing in the future. As with any treatment program, some of you may not have been successful in reducing your fear or phobia. If you feel this way and don't know how to improve your program, then you may want to consider work with a professional counselor or therapist. In such cases it is advisable to contact a professional who knows about relaxation training and the kind of program you have been using. Do not feel embarrassed or uncomfortable about seeking professional help. *And you shouldn't feel discouraged either.* A therapist is someone who can help set up a new program to successfully eliminate your fear or phobia. Your therapist may even suggest useful alterations in the present program. The important point to realize is that failing at a self-administered treatment does *not* mean you are unable to change.

Those of you who have benefited from treatment may still want to do additional work. In line with the previous examples, you may want to focus on relaxation skills to further reduce feelings of physical tension. Additional practice with coping self-statements could also be useful. Some of you may even have a second fear or phobia that you want to eliminate. You can do this by reapplying the principles of your first program to the new goal. The second time around, your program will probably go more quickly, since you already have relaxation skills and you are familiar with the principles of gradual approach.

At this point, your written program has accomplished all that it can. You have learned the principles for fear reduction currently judged most effective, and you have systematically applied them to your particular problem. Before you put this book away, would you take a few minutes now to assist *me*? On the next page is a short questionnaire you can fill out to let me know how helpful this program was to you. The questionnaire can be cut out of the book and is easy to mail to me.

Please take the time. The information from your questionnaire can be used to revise future editions of this book. In that way, others will benefit from your experience—*and they won't have to be afraid.*

FEEDBACK QUESTIONNAIRE

General Instructions: This questionnaire asks you about your fear or phobia, how the program went, and how you evaluate the treatment. Do *NOT* put your name on the questionnaire; that way you can honestly answer all the questions.

1. Please describe the type of fear or phobia you had:

2. What portions of the treatment program did you complete and how clear do you think the instructions were. Under the headings "Completed?" and "Clear?" please write either (a) totally, (b) partially, or (c) not at all.

Completed?   Clear?

     Step 1: Learning to Relax _____

     Step 2: Planning your Strategy for Approach _____

     Step 3: Overcoming your Fears and Phobias _____

3. Did you find the introductory chapters (Chapters 1-3) interesting and helpful?

4. In Chapter 5 you planned your strategy for approach. At that time you filled out an Assessment Sheet and rated your general level of fear on a scale from 0 to 10. What was the rating you gave? Rating = _____.

5. After treatment (Chapter 7) you again rated your general level of fear. What was your rating then? Rating = _____.

6. Would you say your fear is now (a) totally eliminated? (b) moderately decreased? (c) slightly decreased? (d) unchanged? (e) other? _____

7. Please give specific examples of how your fear or phobia has changed (or not changed): _____

8. Use this part of the questionnaire for general comments on the treatment program. What did you like? What could be improved upon?

_____

_____

_____

_____

_____

HOW TO MAIL BACK THIS QUESTIONNAIRE

When you have completed all the questions, cut the questionnaire out of the book. Then follow steps 1 through 4 as explained below.

_____

1. FOLD ALONG THIS LINE SO THAT THE TOP THIRD OF THE PAGE FOLDS UNDER

2. FOLD ALONG THIS LINE SO THAT THE BOTTOM THIRD OF THE PAGE FOLDS UNDER

3. Place
   Stamp
   Here

Gerald M. Rosen, Ph.D.
P.O. Box 25865
Seattle, Washington 98125

4. STAPLE OR TAPE HERE AND DROP QUESTIONNAIRE IN MAILBOX

CUT QUESTIONNAIRE OUT OF BOOK ALONG THIS LINE

REFERENCES

The treatment program presented in this book is primarily based on procedures developed in the 1950s by Dr. Joseph Wolpe, M.D. Dr. Wolpe called his technique *systematic desensitization*—probably because the treatment teaches people to "systematically" reduce or "desensitize" their fears and anxieties. Relevant books by Dr. Wolpe include the following:

Psychotherapy by reciprocal inhibition. Stanford, Calif.: Stanford University Press, 1958.

The practice of behavior therapy (2nd ed.). New York: Pergamon Press, 1973.

Since Dr. Wolpe's original writings, researchers have carefully studied the extent to which systematic desensitization can eliminate fears and phobias; they have also tried to explain why the technique is apparently effective. A list of individual studies on these issues would be prohibitively long; therefore, only a selected group of review materials is cited below. As you can see, even the reviews are numerous. You will also notice that the reviews generally appear in professional journals; these are likely to be found in libraries associated with colleges, universities, or medical schools.

Borkovec, T. The role of expectancy and physiological feedback in fear research: A review with special reference to subject characteristics. *Behavior Therapy*, 1973, 4, 491-505.

Davison, G. C., & Wilson, G. T. Processes of fear reduction in systematic desensitization: Cognitive and social reinforcement factors in humans. *Behavior Therapy*, 1973, 4, 1-21.

Franks, C.M. (Ed.) *Behavior therapy: Appraisal and status.* New York: McGraw-Hill, 1969 (see chapters by G.L. Paul and P.J. Lang).

Lick, J., & Bootzin, R. Expectancy factors in the treatment of fear: Methodological and theoretical issues. *Psychological Bulletin,* 1975, *82*, 917-931.

Mathews, A.M. Psychophysiological approaches to the investigation of desensitization and related procedures. *Psychological Bulletin,* 1971, *76*, 73-91.

Rosen, G. M., Subjects' initial therapeutic expectancies and subjects' awareness of therapeutic goals in systematic desensitization: A review. *Behavior Therapy,* 1976, *7*, 14-27.

Van Egeren, L. F. Psychophysiological aspects of systematic desensitization: Some outstanding issues. *Behaviour Research and Therapy,* 1971. *9*, 65-77.

Wilson, G. T., & Davison, G. C. Processes of fear reduction in systematic desensitization: Animal studies. *Psychological Bulletin,* 1971, *76*, 1-14.

As you can see from their titles, the above reviews generally focus solely on the technique of systematic desensitization. For the reader who wants a broader overview of the area, I strongly recommend the following references by Dr. Isaac Marks. His writings provide the clearest analysis I am aware of for understanding fears and their treatment.

It should be noted that the treatment program presented in this book includes several departures from the original procedures developed by Dr. Wolpe. Justification for these changes can be found in the writings of Dr. Marks and in the previously cited reviews.

Fears and Phobias. New York: Academic Press, 1969. Behavioral treatments of phobic and obsessive-compulsive disorders: A critical appraisal. In M. Hersen, R.M. Eisler, & P.M. Miller (Eds.), *Progress in behavior modification: Volume 1.* New York: Academic Press, 1975.

In the 1960s it was shown that parts of the procedures developed by Dr. Wolpe could be "automated"; the presence of a therapist was not essential and patients successfully eliminated fears and phobias with the help of tape recorded instructions, records, and even computer programs. Such findings suggested the possibility that people could self-administer their treatment if they had access to adequate instructional materials. The following treatment studies have since demonstrated this to be the case.

Baker, B.L., Cohen, D.C., & Saunders, J.T. Self-directed desensitization for acrophobia. *Behaviour Research and Therapy,* 1973, *11,* 79-89.

Clark, F. Self-administered desensitization. *Behaviour Research and Therapy,* 1973, *11,* 335-338.

Kahn, M., & Baker, B. Desensitization with minimal therapist contact. *Journal of Abnormal Psychology,* 1968. *73,* 198-200.

Marshall, W.L., Presse, L., & Andrews, W.R. A self-administered program for public speaking anxiety. *Behaviour Research and Therapy.* 1976, 14, 33-40.

Morris, L.W., & Thomas, C.R. Treatment of phobias by a self-administered desensitization technique. *Journal of Behavior Therapy and Experimental Psychiatry,* 1973, *4,* 397-399.

Phillips, R.E., Johnson, G.D., & Geyer, A. Self-administered sysmatic desensitization. *Behaviour Research and Therapy,* 1972, *10,* 93-96.

Repucci, N.D., & Baker, B.L. Self-desensitization: Implications for treatment and teaching. In R.D. Rubin & C.M. Franks (Eds.), *Advances in behavior therapy*, New York: Academic Press, 1969.

Rosen, G.M., Glasgow, R.E., & Barrera, M., Jr. A controlled study to assess the clinical efficacy of totally self-administered systematic desensitization. *Journal of Consulting and Clinical Psychology*, 1976, 44, 208-217.

For those of you interested in the general area of self-help treatments, there are several books and articles you may want to consider:

Goldfried, M.R., & Merbaum, M. *Behavior change through self-control*. New York: Holt, Rinehart, and Winston, 1973.

Mahoney, M.J., & Thoresen, C.E. *Self-control: Power to the person*. Monterey, Calif.: Brooks/Cole, 1974.

Rosen, G.M. The development and use of nonprescription behavior therapies. *American Psychologist*, 1976, *31*, 139-141.

Thoresen, C.E., & Coates, T.J. Behavioral self-control: Some clinical concerns. In M. Hersen, R.M. Eisler, & P.M. Miller (Eds.), *Progress in behavior modification* (Vol 2.). New York: Academic Press, in press.

Thoresen, C.E., & Mahoney, M.J. *Behavioral self-control*. New York: Holt, Rinehart, and Winston, 1974.